Praise for
This Is Me and *Watch Th*

"*This Is Me* will encourage, inspire, and challenge anyone who dives in. Many girls and women feel too scared or uncomfortable to talk about these issues with a guy. For that reason, this book poses a uniqueness that separates it from the pack. Not only is Jeffrey's approach on a very personal level, it's packed with biblical truths. This book will change your life if you're a young lady, a mother, or even a guy!"

—JOSH REEDY, lead singer, DecembeRadio

"In *Watch This,* Jeffrey uses biblical truth to encourage teen guys to grow toward authentic manhood."

—JASON ROY, lead singer, Building 429

"Jeffrey Dean has a way of zeroing in on today's youth culture. He knows teens and how to communicate the love of Jesus to them in a way that captures their attention and convicts their hearts."

—JOSH D. MCDOWELL, author and communicator

"Jeffrey Dean's *This Is Me* reads like an honest conversation with a trusted big brother. No catchy gimmicks or watered-down lessons—just straight talk about the things girls care about most, backed up by Scripture, with all the authenticity that today's teens long for. I can't wait to share it with the girls in my life!"

—SHELLEY BREEN, singer, Point of Grace, and
of *Life, Love, and Other My*

"In both *This Is Me* and *Wa* eat job of identifying the things that a mes-
sage of hope for teens. His w strong. You'll love what you read, because it conn with the very heart of God."

—DANIEL S. WOLGEMUTH, President/CEO, Youth for Christ

"*This Is Me* is one of the most thorough, honest, biblical, and compassionate books I have read in quite some time. It's the kind of message I believe God will use to touch many teenagers across America. Jeffrey Dean is not only a talented musician and communicator, but God has given him a deep love for today's teenagers, and it shows. I highly recommend his work to you."

—DAWSON MCALLISTER, national talk show host

"Among student communicators I've heard, I rate Jeffrey Dean among the top five. His message is relevant, clear, and biblical. He has a unique ability to relate to students about their culture and the choices they face. I highly recommend him."

—PHIL WALDREP, Phil Waldrep Ministries, Trinity, Alabama

"Jeffrey is a gifted and passionate speaker who connects with teens at all levels. He is insightful and relevant—speaking into today's issues with the boldness that contemporary student culture requires."

—RON KECK, managing director, Serendipity House Publishing

"I am always amazed at the energy and enthusiasm that Jeffrey Dean brings to his work with teens. And his enthusiasm is contagious! Jeffrey's abstinence message has been an extremely valuable resource for our clubs—becoming, in fact, the perfect vehicle to carry this all-important message to our young people. I know first-hand that Jeffrey's message is not only getting into our schools and youth facilities, but it's being listened to and taken to heart by kids."

—JOHN HOLLIS, director of development, Boys and Girls Clubs of Delaware

"Jeffrey's stories are true, his facts are accurate, and his message to teens about making today's choices count for the future is heard loud and clear."

—LESLEE J. UNRUH, president of the Abstinence Clearinghouse

watch this

a getting-there guide to manhood for teen guys

jeffrey dean

MULTNOMAH
BOOKS

WATCH THIS
PUBLISHED BY MULTNOMAH BOOKS
12265 Oracle Boulevard, Suite 200
Colorado Springs, Colorado 80921
A division of Random House Inc.

ISBN 978-1-59052-984-3

Library of Congress Cataloging-in-Publication Data
Dean, Jeffrey.
Watch this : a getting-there guide to manhood for teen guys / by Jeffrey Dean. — 1st ed.
p. cm.
ISBN 978-1-59052-984-3
1. Teenage boys—Religious life. 2. Teenage boys—Conduct of life. I. Title.
BV4541.3.D43 2007
248.8'32—dc22

2007010433

Printed in the United States of America
2007—First Edition

10 9 8 7 6 5 4 3 2 1

To Mom and Dad
Thank you for encouraging me to dream

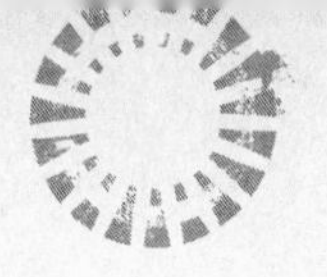

Contents

Acknowledgments

Many thanks to everyone at Multnomah: To my editor, Adrienne Spain, you are truly a gift. Thank you for your commitment to this project. To David Kopp, executive editor, for our new friendship and for your immeasurable wisdom. To Jason Myhre and Tiffany Lauer, marketing directors, for believing.

Thank you to the many who have journeyed with us over the past decade of ministry to teens and their families. Special thanks to Kimberly and Dan Klaver—you know my love!

To all my family, and especially Kent and Jeremy, for all the great stories we've made in life so far. I love you like brothers...oh yeah, you are my brothers. To my girls—you are my joy. To my wife, you are everything.

To God. Thank you for taking control of my life and saying, "Watch this!"

1

Real Men Stand

What would it take to show the world the real you?

I still remember how it felt standing at the top of "the Big One." Long before halfpipes and vert ramps, we simply had this steep, daunting hill. The journey down the Big One was the only way home from the neighborhood swimming pool, so for us there were only two ways down: walk or ride.

At the end of each day we'd stand gazing down the Mount Everest of blacktop, and then, one by one, the others would launch their boards until I was the only one left, standing alone with my board and a stomach full of fear. That's when I would finally take off down the hill…sitting on my board. It took about fifteen seconds to actually make it down. But it only took five or six seconds for the insults to start flying.

"Stand up! Stand up, you sissy!" the other boarders would yell.

There was a protocol, the unwritten riding rule, and we all knew it. Stand, or be:

- a boarding baby
- a sissy skater
- a sitter

Anyone could sit down while surfing the Big One. That was easy. But it took a "man" to be willing to stand and conquer the holy hill, the supersurfing slope, the four-wheel ride of royalty, the… Okay, you get it.

Anyway, as a kid, I was not only afraid of heights, wasps, sleeping in the dark, and my older brother's fist, I was also afraid of standing on a fifteen-by-five-inch orange plastic board on wheels as it traveled much faster than I dared, especially since, somewhere between the top and the bottom of the paved slope, I could experience real pain. So it didn't take long for me to be labeled a "skating sissy."

Brad, Eric, Steve, others whose names I can't remember, and, of course, my older brother were just a few of our neighborhood boarding heroes who had mastered the Big One. Day after day they would sit poolside, bragging about their downhill dominance. I dreamed of having the courage to graduate from sitter to stander. Then *I* would have bragging rights and, most important, the respect of my older brother.

I'm not sure what made me decide to finally attempt to stand, but it might've had something to do with the fact that the Schubert twins, Laura and Leslie, who lived in our neighborhood and whose home was directly at the bottom of the Big One, were looking particularly lovely that summer day. They were watching, and they knew what it meant to stand. They knew about the boarding heroes. And unfortunately for me, they also knew that I was a sitter. I had to do something about that.

hit pause

Have you ever had one of those moments where you envisioned the finish line and everyone was there chanting your name as you were the first to cross? or that moment in the final seconds of the big game when the score is tied and the ball's in your hands? or the Hail Mary spiral that's thrown into the end zone as the final second ticks off the clock and your hands and the ball meet at just the right moment, and then you're hoisted onto the shoulders of your teammates, and everyone is cheering for you, including that hot girl you've been checking out at school?

So I did it. I positioned my lead foot, I shifted my weight forward, and I pushed off. I guess it was somewhere around the seventh or eighth second that I realized I was moving much faster than I wanted to be moving. And just as quickly, I realized I no longer cared what Brad, Eric, Steve, my brother, or even the Schubert twins thought. Shortly after that moment of enlightenment, the pain began. I'm not exactly sure which body part met the pavement first, but eventually every inch of me got a closeup view.

Becoming one with the pavement is an experience unlike most I've encountered, one I hoped I'd never encounter again. But I did. Three days later. Same hill, same board, similar pain. I was determined to conquer that hill standing, with all my doubters watching. I never did. All I ended up with when summer was over were a few more bloody knees, skinned-up palms, and a scar on my arm that's still there to this day.

think about it

If I'd said no that day atop the Big One and made my way down the hill sitting on my board, would that have made me any less of a man? Or if I'd successfully surfed the hill standing rather than kissed the pavement, would I be a better man today?

Hindsight tells me that attempting to master the hill wasn't the smartest thing I've ever done. But we do some really dumb things when we're trying to earn other people's approval. I wanted to become something more than I was. I wanted everyone to watch what I could do, to see how I could accomplish something awesome. And I thought conquering the Big One was the way to show them.

Watch This

Take a minute to look really deep into your heart and then consider these questions:

- Do I want more from life than what I've got right now?
- Am I unfulfilled?
- Do I feel like something is missing from my life?
- Is there something inside of me that wants to be more, to not settle for just getting by?
- Can I be a better man than I am right now?

If you said yes to any one of those questions, then this book is for you. *Watch This* is a guide to becoming more, to finding that "something missing," to becoming a man of God. The desire that led me to sacrifice my body on the Big One all those times was one most of us share as men: We want to take risks, show off, and *win.* We want to say "Watch this!" to the world and then accomplish something awesome.

What I didn't realize was, my desire could be channeled into a better purpose—an eternal, God-given purpose. This book is meant to give you the tools first to find God's purpose for you, and then to show the world what God can do through you. And as you work to follow him, *God* will be watching. And you'll get way more than earthly praise. Check it out:

> His master replied, "Well done, good and faithful servant! You have been faithful with a few things; I will put you in charge of many things. Come and share your master's happiness!" (Matthew 25:21)

Whatever pride and prizes you could've gotten by winning on your own, none of them will be as rewarding as what the Creator of the universe can give you when you live for him.

So, do you want to learn how to do that?

It's not as impossible as you might think. All you've got to do is trust the Man who made you. Because he:

- wants to transform you into something better than what the world says you should be
- has created you for a specific reason
- wants to develop in you the qualities necessary to do great things for him
- is at work in your life to give you a future beyond anything you can imagine

All the aspects of your life—dilemmas, temptations, celebrations, struggles, and choices—are coming together to uniquely make you into the man God wants to use, if you choose to let him.

The World's Standards or God's?

I may not have realized it at the time, but failing to conquer that hill taught me a valuable lesson. I learned that pleasing other people is not what makes me a man. Being a man isn't about always winning, always being strong, always impressing the girls. Being a real man has nothing to do with this world's rules and everything to do with God's rules. I learned that being a man is not about standing when others demand it, expect it, or suggest it. Being a man is about standing for what you know is right. And, more importantly, standing for what God says is right.

The problem is that what other people think of us feels really important. It did to me. It still does sometimes. It seems like people are always watching, judging, and criticizing, and you just want to prove to them that you're good enough. But as long as you're judging yourself by the world's standards, you're always going to fall short. The world's rules are harsh and unforgiving, and they're always the same:

- You lose? Game over.
- You don't have the game? Sit on the bench.
- You can't make the grades? You don't pass.
- You aren't who everyone else wants you to be? You're not accepted.
- You don't meet their standards? You're out.

- You don't look the way they do? You're not invited.
- You can't stand? You're just a sitter.

I remember meeting fifteen-year-old Michael while speaking at a conference. He approached me one night, and we talked for a long time about his home life, his friends, and the fact that he felt extremely lonely. Michael had friends. But only because "I started partying and drinking with them." He said, "I really wasn't popular until I started living like they all lived... And now I'm not even sure who I am anymore."

I totally understand what he's saying. My attempts to conquer the Big One and Michael's desire to find genuine friendships are similar because we were both in search of the same thing: fulfillment. You can probably relate to that. We all want to feel accepted, appreciated, respected, and loved. And like Michael, even with the best of intentions, it can be easy to replace God's standards with the world's.

You're a teenager, just starting to become a man, and this means you're going to have to make some tough decisions. Satan is working overtime to convince you that, unless you find acceptance and popularity in the world and measure up to the world's standards, you'll never find true fulfillment. You were created to find purpose in God, but Satan wants to convince you that God isn't as cool as what the world has to offer. He'll probably slip these ideas in without you even noticing. He's great at getting us to see lies as truth, the world's way as the right way.

When you accept Christ as your Savior, you become God's ambassador to the world. People will be watching. And what will they see? A boy performing for the world, or a man performing

God's will in his life? Lasting fulfillment will never be found in anything this world offers. If you're not careful, you can quickly and unintentionally buy into the world's definition of manhood. But if you live by the world's rules, you're always going to feel like you're not quite good enough. You'll always be looking for more. Fortunately, God operates by a different standard.

Adult or Man?

Right now you're going through all the cliché teenager things—your body is changing, your voice is deepening, and older people are always exclaiming about how much you've grown. But becoming a man is not just about growing older. (I'm sure you can think of a few people older than you who don't act like "men" at all.) You don't choose whether or not you get older—you just do. But becoming a man is a choice.

think about it

How do you choose to become a man?

- By being more responsible for the choices you make—even the ones no one knows about but you.
- By carefully considering what kind of music you download into your head.
- By stopping to process possible consequences of an important choice before making it.
- By choosing friends wisely and then being a good friend to them.

- By respecting the wishes of your parents, even when you disagree with them.
- By taking ownership of your relationship with God by committing to spend more time talking with him.
- By living so that those who are watching will see God in you.

Everything that's happened in your life until this exact moment has been orchestrated by God. He has allowed every moment of glory, defeat, celebration, tragedy, happiness, and disappointment. Nothing that's happened in your life has been a surprise to him. And there's no part of your life he doesn't know about. He knows:

- your greatest struggles
- your disappointments
- your home life
- your fears
- what you're thinking at this very moment
- the choices you regret
- what you do in your private world
- what you hope for
- what you dream of
- absolutely everything about you

Even before you drew your first breath, God knew you. And ever since, he has had his hand on every aspect of your life. He knows you better than you know yourself, and he even knows things you don't know about yourself. The Bible says, "Even the very hairs of your head are all numbered" (Matthew 10:30).

God knows so much about you because he cares so much about you. He did create you, after all. He has an incredible plan for your life—and he wants you to know about it. It may not take something as big as a hill, a skateboard, and pain to get your attention—but it did for me. And God will do whatever's necessary to get you to focus on him, because he wants you to fully experience the life he's created for you.

the real deal

God knows your potential. He gave it to you. He understands your weaknesses. He sees past your inabilities. He has complete confidence in the man you can be. Only God can help you reach your potential. Only he can give you strength beyond your weaknesses. Only he can give you lasting fulfillment. But your attention has to be on him, not on measuring up to others. And if you're focusing on the wrong things, he may use extreme measures to get your attention.

Carrying out the game plan God has drawn up for you will make you feel more fulfilled than anything in this world. But before you can experience that, you have to trust him.

Proverbs 3:5–6 reads, "Trust in the LORD with all your heart and lean not on your own understanding; in all your ways acknowledge him, and he will make your paths straight."

In other words, God is saying:

Give me a chance. Let me prove to you that I have it all under control.

Let me show you that I am capable of doing something amazing with your life.

Let me make you into the man I created you to be.

Let me make you into the man who will stand for me.

Let me use you to show the world who I am.

What You Need to Know as You Read

This book is meant to help you grow into the man God created you to be—the one who trusts him and stands for him, the one who helps a watching, waiting world to see him. But before you start reading, there are four Foundational Truths you need to know. These four things will help you get the most out of what I'm sharing with you—and I hope they will help you get the most out of your life too.

1. Don't just take my word for it.

When I was younger and I read certain books that used a lot of scripture, I would skip over the scripture. If you do that with this book, you'll miss the good stuff. Each verse has been chosen for a very specific reason. So as you read, don't just take my word on a particular issue. Read the included scriptures. Think about them. Go deeper. Ask questions. Don't just be challenged by me, be challenged by God in his Word.

2. If he says it, he means it.

Since I just established in Truth #1 that I'll share a ton of scriptures with you throughout this book, you need to know this: if

God says it, he means it. There are some who teach that God's Word is no longer relevant to your life or that you don't have to do everything the Bible says. Don't buy it. The Bible is truth. It's from God. And it's God's gift to you to guide you on your journey. Without it, you would be just as lost as Tony Hawk without his board. The point is—you can take God at his Word.

3. No wimps allowed.

This book is not for wimps. You don't have to do everything that's written in the following pages. But you'll have a hard time becoming the man God says you can be if you don't. This book is not a walk-in-the-park, feel-good read. Becoming a man of God is serious business. Representing God in this world means lots of people will be watching you—and that's a big responsibility. So as you read, you'll need discipline, consistency, determination, and trust. And if you choose to apply these truths to your life, it's a choice that'll help transform you into his likeness and shape you into the man you were made to be.

4. You can do this.

I'm going to be honest with you and really challenge you in these next chapters. I'll ask things of you that are more difficult than anything you've done before. But don't worry—though you can't become the man God wants you to be by just cramming for the test the night before, the extra work will be worth it. There may be times as you're reading when you'll feel like throwing in the towel. But don't do it. Your walk with God isn't like getting a shot of a spiritual steroid. It's a one-day-at-a-time thing. So don't give up. You can do this.

Why You Need to Keep Reading

First, God wants to guide you as you become a man, but you might need some help hearing his voice and understanding his Word. My hope is that this book will help you follow him where he wants you to go and do what he wants you to do. As you start really working at this and begin to see yourself as he sees you, all those problems that weigh you down every day will feel a little lighter because you don't have to deal with them alone.

Second, this book will also be a resource for you. Use it as one. You'll face problems that seem insurmountable. And Satan will work overtime to mess up God's plan for your life. That's why I've devoted an entire chapter to each of these critical areas:

- family
- friendships
- dating
- sex
- pornography and masturbation (yep, we're gonna talk about *that*)
- evangelism

You probably have a lot of questions about the stuff in that list. Maybe you're too embarrassed to ask anyone else, or maybe you don't know who to ask. Hopefully this book will be a place you can come to for answers. Inside all these chapters, I'll try to use my experience working with teenagers to answer some of your toughest questions. I won't pretend that I know everything—because I definitely don't—but I'll share what I've learned in my own walk with God and in helping other people with theirs.

This is your moment of decision. Right now you're standing

at the top of the Big One, and the question is, what'll you do? Will you shrink back when the challenge comes and not even try to stand? Or will you accept the challenge and let the world watch what God can do in your life?

If you choose option two, you'll stand for God in a world that desperately needs to see him and know him. And you will see God go to work in your life in amazing ways...

You just watch.

2

You're Not a Dog, Man

What to do when you're surrounded by actors and animals.

Each spring MTV broadcasts live on a beach in Florida, California, or someplace where there's a lot of sun, surf, and sand. There's only one rule that applies: no rules. Nothing to stop those college guys from drinking until they vomit. Nothing keeping them from sleeping with that strange girl in the string bikini whose name they never asked for. Nothing holding them back from doing all the things a "man" should want to do.

Stop and consider how men are usually portrayed on TV, in magazines, and in movies. Write down five characteristics that best describe what *man* means in today's culture.

1.

2.

3.

4.

5.

What words did you choose? Were they positive or negative? Maybe they were a little bit of both.

When it comes to what's cool, it seems like *man* has nothing to do with qualities that are good, pure, and honorable. He's just a self-centered, egotistical jerk who's only concerned with partying, drinking, and sex. He's a dog who can't control his canine cravings, constantly on the hunt for a chick and a doggie bowl full of beer. And, weirdly, men seem very proud of that.

When it comes to making the right choices, countless commercials, movies, and sitcoms send the message that real men just simply roll over and play dead. Why is that? Is it that men are no longer capable of exercising self-control? Is it that there's no need for men to be respectful? Or is it that they don't know there's a higher purpose to live for?

We men have become confused about who we are, what our role is, and how we live out that role. Men have bought the lie that they're supposed to be tough, emotionless, and sex-crazed—never caring, responsible, or moral. We've accepted that life is about doing whatever we want, whenever we want—when it's really about so much more than that.

Kevin was one such man. I met him recently at a teen conference where I spoke. He was a Christian, had been active in church since wearing Huggies, and was seen as a leader by the members of his youth group. But Kevin admitted to me that his life was far from God-honoring. Most Friday-night postgame parties began with alcohol and ended with a hookup. He couldn't remember the last time he'd actually read his Bible apart from Sunday school, and his private life consisted mostly of a secret addiction to well-endowed girls on his computer screen.

Kevin had Jesus living in his heart. But like many Christian guys, he was completely clueless about how to make that relationship more than just a Sunday ritual. And he's not the only one with this problem. Not by a long shot.

After more than a decade of teen ministry, I'm convinced there are a lot of Christian guys who want to live right but don't put into practice the everyday steps that make living right more than a desire. And if you don't put your faith into practice, you've missed the point, because Christ doesn't just want you to know him. He wants you to help other people know him too, through what you say *and* how you live.

To become the man God sees you can be, first you have to realize that nothing this world can offer you will ever make you a complete man. Not parties or girls or sex, even if that stuff seems like so much fun that you couldn't possibly need anything else.

I'm convinced—even if you're not just yet—that you really do want more. More than what Kevin was experiencing, more than what MTV touts as the real world. You *do* want the best in life. You *do* want to rise above the mediocrity and find lasting fulfillment as a man. You *do* want to show everyone what Christ can do in the world. In your mind you know what's right. But like lots of guys, you just need to know how to make it stick in your heart.

To find out how to do this, you have to stop making excuses for the poor choices you've made and start making a difference with your life. A crucial step in this realization is knowing who you are in God's eyes.

Know Who You Are

Who are you? Write down several qualities that define who you are.

Never fully understanding who you are will always leave you wanting to be someone else.

Never fully understanding who you are will always lead you to try to be something you are not.

Never fully understanding who you are will always leave you being something less than who you can be.

In this world, it seems almost impossible to define who you are by what should really matter:

- who created you
- what God thinks of you
- how God sees you
- the plan God has for you

Because everything and everyone around you are saying who you are is based on:

- your popularity
- your appearance
- your wealth
- your job
- your car
- your body
- your possessions

Living for that stuff may bring some momentary pleasure and give you a temporary sense of value. But it won't last. (You've probably already experienced that a few times.) Focusing on those superficial things will always make you confused about who you are. And when one of them fails to satisfy, you'll feel the need to reinvent yourself as you look for another "thing" to help you find a sense of self-worth.

If you're going to become the man God wants you to be, you have to understand clearly who you are in his eyes. Why? Because your choices are a reflection of who you are. If you don't see yourself as God sees you, you'll keep making the wrong choices, and you'll never be able to fully embrace and live out the life you were created to experience.

I didn't realize, as I stood atop the Big One debating whether to be a stander or a sitter, that the issue for me was nothing more than confusion about who I was. I guess you could say I was faking it.

Skateboarding was the cool thing in my neighborhood. It seemed not only that everyone was doing it but that everyone except me was doing it well. I thought I had to be what everyone else said I should be. Therefore, I thought I had to do what everyone else was doing. And in the end, my reward was pain. A lot of pain.

What about you? Are you faking it?

A faker: has to work hard trying to make and keep friends.

The real you: never has to work so hard to get and keep the attention of others.

A faker: bases his value on what others think.

The real you: bases his value on what God says.

A faker: has to keep reinventing himself to feel secure.

The real you: finds his security in God.

A faker: has to do things he doesn't always agree with in order to feel accepted.

The real you: never compromises his convictions for anyone.

hit pause

Consider the life you're living.

- Have you altered your appearance, the way you dress, the music you listen to, or the parties you attend because of a friend?
- Are you spending less time reading the Bible and talking with God?
- Have you done something you never thought you'd do—had a drink, smoked, done drugs, hooked up with a girl—because you thought it would make you more popular?

Living as a faker will never satisfy you. Living as a faker means you'll always feel the need to change who you are. Living as a faker will always leave you wanting to be something or someone else.

If you're faking it, you're living a lie. The only way to start living as the real you is to find out how God sees you—and learn how to see yourself that way too. Because you are *exactly* who God made you to be.

What does God see when he sees you? Look at Genesis 1:27:

God created man in his own image,
in the image of God he created him.

1. The real you—you're God's mirror.

What do you think it means to be God's mirror?

Being God's mirror means that you actually have the ability to reflect the character of God in how you live your life—as you think, act, reason, discern, talk, and interact with others. This means that when others see you, they see God.

It's important for you to understand that you're created in the image of God because knowing this will be the foundation for your self-worth. You won't be able to let others see God in you until *you* can see God in you. Realizing God made you to be like him proves how much God thought of you when he created you. You may not like who you are. You may not feel very valuable. But God believes your value is immeasurable. That's why he created you. You're valuable to him, so valuable that of all the incredible things he created on earth, only one—humankind—was created in his image.

As you're reading this book, understanding this truth—that you're God's mirror in the world—will be very important for you to remember. Being able to reflect God's character means you're also capable of honoring God in every area of your life, from how you talk to your parents to how you deal with sex and dating, from what you do when everyone's watching to what you do when no one's looking.

2. The real you—you are good.

Look at what God says about you in Genesis 1:31:

> God looked over everything he had made;
> it was so good, so very good! (MSG)

In this passage of Scripture, God has just finished creating all things. I can barely imagine that moment when God looks out at all the wonders of his creation. And what is his first response? "It is good!" In other words, he's saying, "I am pleased with *all* I've made." And, yes, that includes you.

How awesome is it to know that God, the Creator of all things, looks at you and says, "You are good"? You can't get a better endorsement than that.

Because his creation of you is good, you have the ability to be good, do good, and thus live a life that reflects him. Knowing you are good in God's eyes should lift a big weight off your shoulders. No more struggling to meet the world's impossible expectations—because you've already received the greatest honor and basis for self-worth.

No Way

Come on, Jeffrey, you've got to be kidding. I'm not good. I do mean, stupid stuff all the time. I've screwed up so much, I don't think God can use me anyway.

I hear you. I don't know what you've done, but I understand what you're saying. It's hard to feel like you're worthy when all you can think about is all the bad things you've done.

the Truth

Oh yes, you shaped me first inside, then out;
you formed me in my mother's womb.
I thank you, High God—you're breathtaking!
Body and soul, I am marvelously made!
I worship in adoration—what a creation!
You know me inside and out,
you know every bone in my body;
You know exactly how I was made, bit by bit,
how I was sculpted from nothing into something.
Like an open book, you watched me grow from
conception to birth;
all the stages of my life were spread out before you,
The days of my life all prepared
before I'd even lived one day. (Psalm 139:13–16, MSG)

But try something for me. Think about the choice you've made that you regret the most. Focus on it. Now, think about this—right at this very minute God knows about that thing you regret doing more than anything. And he *still* thinks you're good. Seriously, if you ask for forgiveness for what you did, it's like it didn't even happen. God just erases it. You *are* good because God made you that way—and with his grace, he keeps making you that way every day.

Write down five good characteristics about yourself. Then, beside each characteristic, write how you can use each to honor God with your life.

1.

2.

3.

4.

5.

3. The real you—you're a man of responsibility.

God created Adam and Eve to live in the Garden of Eden, and life in the garden must have been pretty sweet. Adam had everything he could ever want: a place to live, no rent, no bills, all the food he wanted, a beautiful backyard, a wife. And since clothes weren't even invented yet, the best part of all was that he didn't have to worry about getting dressed—ever. He did have some other responsibilities, though. At creation, God outlined one important role that Adam, and every man since Adam, was called to fulfill:

> So GOD formed from the dirt of the ground all the animals of the field and all the birds of the air. He brought them to the Man to see what he would name them. Whatever the Man called each living creature, that was its name. The Man named the cattle, named the birds of the air, named the wild animals. (Genesis 2:19–20, MSG)

God gave Adam *responsibility.* He made Adam responsible for every creature that walked the planet. Now, those are some big shoes to fill. Okay, Adam didn't wear shoes then, but you get the point. Adam was the original King of the Hill, and he was given full reign. But God didn't simply say, "Here are the keys to the place, the fridge is full, the car's loaded with gas, so party on," did he? Of course not. He said, "I'm giving you the privilege of being responsible for all of my creation. Don't blow it, don't abuse it. You're a man. Use this privilege wisely."

The responsibility placed on Adam by God has also been handed down to you. So think about this: are you being responsible? You've been created as a leader, as a man of responsibility—not to just do whatever the heck you want, but to use your abilities, gifts, and individuality wisely.

hit pause

If I showed up at your house tonight and you and I could pop some corn, pour a couple of Cokes, and throw in a sixty-minute DVD summarizing the last year of your life, what would we see? What would you want us to be able to see?

Do you see yourself as:

- a man who reflects God?
- a man who is good?
- a man of responsibility?

If you really want to know how you see yourself, just take a look at the life you're living—because you live what you believe.

If you don't see yourself as a man bearing God's image, you'll never live your life as a mirror that lets others see God in you.

If you don't see yourself as a good man uniquely created by him, then you'll never fully use your goodness to live out the life he planned for you.

If you don't see yourself as a man of great responsibility, you'll most likely live a life foolishly wasting your individuality, time, and abilities.

When you start seeing yourself as God sees you, then you'll begin living a life worthy of the One who made you—instead of living like some hound on a hunt for a good time.

My Space

Write a prayer asking that God will help you see yourself as he sees you. Then ask God to help you live out your life every day as the man he wants you to be.

3

Playing Hide-and-Seek with God

Trying to fool him comes naturally, but that doesn't mean it's smart.

When I was a kid, I loved to play hide-and-seek. My older brother and I would play it for hours, and we learned to get very creative when finding a place to hide. I remember one time finding what I thought was the perfect hiding place—so perfect my brother never found me. At least that's what I thought.

After hiding for more than forty-five minutes, I eventually decided to come out of my hiding place and gracefully let him surrender and admit the fact that his younger brother was the best hider. That is, until I found him watching TV in the living room. He wasn't even looking for me. Cheap trick.

I'm a lot older now, but I still play that kids' game. My little girls love to play hide-and-seek, especially my youngest, Brynnan. Except she doesn't fully understand the game. When I get done counting to ten, I shout, "Ready or not, here I come!" And it never fails that I find her facing a corner, standing in full view, covering her face with her hands. She can't see me, so she assumes I can't see her either.

Hide-and-seek is a game of pursuit. The rules are simple. Someone hides. Someone pursues. Believe it or not, the game of hide-and-seek has been around for a long time, actually since the beginning of time. The first couple to call earth home played the game. Except, for them, it wasn't a game at all. It was real life. And the stakes were extremely high. Their choice to hide set in motion a pursuit, not only of them, but of all humankind—a pursuit by God.

As you become a man, it's important that you clearly understand this: you're being pursued—and it's God who's pursuing you. Ever since sin number one was committed on earth, God has been in pursuit of every person who's walked this planet. And he's pursuing you because he wants a real relationship with you.

In the last chapter, I said that the real you, the person God made you to be, is defined by three important things: bearing God's image, goodness, and responsibility.

When you read that list, did you want to run to God or hide from him? Were you ashamed because you haven't lived up to God's expectations? Maybe you thought, *God made me to bear his image, but all I do is make him look bad.* Or *God made me to be good, but I've done so many bad things.* Or *God wants me to be responsible, but I'm always just doing things without thinking and screwing stuff up.*

Feeling like you've let God down can make you ashamed. It can make you believe that you don't deserve to have a relationship with him. That shame can make you want to hide from him. But you can't hide from God. And you shouldn't feel like you need to.

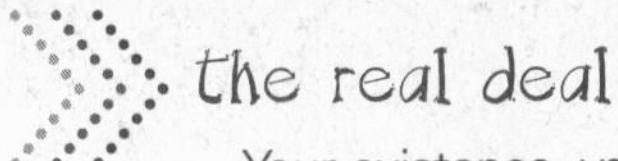

Your existence, value, and purpose as well as God's plan for your life are important enough for him to pursue you.

You Can't Hide from God

Let's check out the story of the first humans who walked planet earth and connect the dots to see how their story set in motion God's pursuit of you. The Bible tells us in Genesis that the Garden of Eden was an awesome place to live. A modern-day Garden of Eden would be like a buffet line of your favorite foods, a 250-inch plasma TV, an unlimited PS3 library of games, ESPN commentators in your backyard, a closet full of the coolest clothes, and hitting the snooze button as much as you want, all wrapped into one. Oh, and there'd be no sadness or murder or any other serious stuff like that. In short, Adam and Eve had everything they could ever want and more. God provided for their every need. But he had one rule: "Don't eat from the tree of the knowledge of good and evil." However, they did exactly what God said not to do.

> The serpent was clever, more clever than any wild animal GOD had made. He spoke to the Woman: "Do I understand that God told you not to eat from any tree in the garden?"
>
> The Woman said to the serpent, "Not at all. We can eat from the trees in the garden. It's only about the tree in the middle of the garden that God said, 'Don't eat from it; don't even touch it or you'll die.' "

> The serpent told the Woman, "You won't die. God knows that the moment you eat from that tree, you'll see what's really going on. You'll be just like God, knowing everything, ranging all the way from good to evil."
>
> When the Woman saw that the tree looked like good eating and realized what she would get out of it—she'd know everything!—she took and ate the fruit and then gave some to her husband, and he ate. (Genesis 3:1–6, MSG)

Adam and Eve didn't realize it at that moment, but their choice to disobey God and buy the lie that Satan sold them set in motion a ripple effect that has continued to this day: *sin.* Their sin separated us from God. And the pursuit began.

hit pause

Imagine you're standing on a beach holding a glass of water. Just as you're about to take a drink, a large wave rushes over your feet, you lose your balance, and you spill your water into the ocean. Is it possible to reach down and refill your empty glass with exactly the same water that was spilled? Of course not. No matter how many times you tried, you'd never be able to get that exact glass of water back. You'd never be able to return it to its original state. In the garden, Adam and Eve's disobedience to God had the same effect as you spilling your water in the ocean. That first sin completely washed away God's perfect world and humankind's perfect fellowship with him. We can never restore that relationship to the way it was. But, luckily, God can.

> When they heard the sound of God strolling in the garden in the evening breeze, the Man and his Wife hid in the trees of the garden, hid from God.
>
> God called to the Man: "Where are you?"
>
> He said, "I heard you in the garden and I was afraid because I was naked. And I hid." (Genesis 3:8–10, MSG)

Why do you think Adam and Eve tried to hide from God?

As the story goes, after bringing sin into the world, Adam and Eve "realized they were naked" (NIV). Though this is definitely not a funny story, I do find it kind of humorous that two adults covered by nothing more than a few leaves from a tree actually thought they could hide from God. Imagine how silly they must've looked to all those animals, running around naked in the garden, frantically looking for a leaf and a place to hide. This was the first game of hide-and-seek that was ever played. But did Adam and Eve really believe they could succeed in hiding from God?

It's as if they were playing hide-and-seek like my daughter Brynnan, when she stands in a corner and hides her face. Adam and Eve assumed that since they couldn't see God, God couldn't see them either. But he could.

Adam and Eve's response—to run and hide—is similar to how a lot of people respond today. We mess up. We ignore it, deny it, or try to cover it up. We hope that God will just forget about it or that maybe he didn't even see our sin at all. But make no mistake—God is an all-knowing God. There's nothing you can hide from him—and nothing he's not willing to forgive. As God is making you into the man he wants you to be, you need to understand that he sees all and knows all. Nothing—*absolutely nothing*—gets past him.

In the Garden of Eden, what got Adam and Eve in trouble? Was it:

Satan?
the fruit?
rules?
their choice to sin?

Only God's Clothing Fits

After their choice to disobey God, look at what Adam and Eve did next.

> Immediately the two of them did "see what's really going on"—saw themselves naked! They sewed fig

leaves together as makeshift clothes for themselves.
(Genesis 3:7, MSG)

God's original plan for people didn't involve clothing. I know that's hard to imagine now, when having the right clothes is imperative (and not wearing clothes at all would get you into big trouble). Clothes weren't necessary until Adam and Eve sinned and understood what being naked was. Then they thought they could adequately clothe themselves without God's help. But they were wrong. They committed the first fashion blunder on planet earth.

Did you notice what kind of clothing the Bible says Adam and Eve made? Genesis says their attempt at fashion design was nothing more than "makeshift clothes."

download

makeshift (adj.) —a temporary and usually inferior substitute

The important point to grab here is not necessarily the type of clothing they made but the idea that whenever we attempt to replace God's plan with our own, the end result will never last and never satisfy. It'll only be a temporary and inferior substitute.

Adam and Eve's first response, rather than running to God, was to run to the world for a quick fix. Isn't this a typical response for us too?

Your Temptation:		Your Makeshift Clothes:
There are overwhelming circumstances.	·····	You turn to a drink.
Temptations seem too difficult to control.	·····	You check out Internet porn.
Everyone else seems to be doing it.	·····	You become sexually active.
You want to be popular.	·····	You do what everyone else is doing.

"I haven't read my Bible or prayed in over two years!"

I still remember where I was standing when Barry said this to me. Barry was in high school. He came up to me after I'd finished speaking at his church. He told me about all the bad things he'd done in his life. Checking out porn, cheating on tests, lying to his parents, and sleeping with his girlfriend were just a few of the regrettable choices he told me about. He said, "How can you really expect God to love me after all the stuff I've done?"

Barry was hiding. He didn't know it, but he was hiding from God by choosing not to spend time talking to him and reading his Word. And in his attempt to cover up his past, Barry was running from God by clothing himself in lies, an addiction to porn, and a sexual relationship, believing that if he hid long enough, God would just forget about him.

Adam and Eve responded to their choice to sin just like Barry. And the game of hide-and-seek began. But what they didn't know was that there was no way they could ever win. They believed that their makeshift clothing would hide the reality of their sin. But whenever we try to take matters into our hands and rely on the world's help, we always lose.

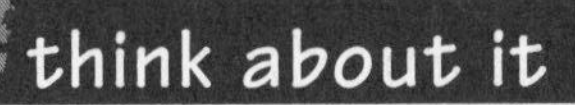

think about it

- Are you hiding behind an inferior substitute now?
- Is God asking something of you that you're not willing to do?
- Are you embracing something in life that's not pleasing to God?
- Are you in a relationship that's not honoring God?
- Do you have a habit or addiction that's pulling you farther away from God?

For now, *it* may seem to be working.

That *thing* may satisfy you today.

She may make you feel good.

It may seem cool to be *It* right now.

But embracing anything other than God's plan for your life will eventually leave you disappointed and unsatisfied.

God has created you for a specific reason. He has a plan for your life. Attempting to find and live out this plan on your own will leave you with nothing more than an inferior substitute that'll eventually fail you, and you'll find yourself running from one leaf of life to the next. Are you wearing makeshift clothes? God wants to dress you in something much better.

Lord of the Seams

After Adam and Eve's initial sin, God could've chosen any number of options:

- End time on earth.
- Kill Adam and Eve.
- Start over with new humans.
- Remove every human's ability to choose.
- Leave Adam and Eve to run around naked until their rears were sunburned.

Once sin occurred, God knew it was only a matter of time before it would happen again. And since humans had free will to choose, God also knew that if he allowed life to continue on earth, every human would have the ability to choose not to love him in return. He could have said, "These humans will never get it right! I should just destroy them before it gets worse."

But have a look at verses 8–10 again and see what God did instead.

> When they heard the sound of GOD strolling in the garden in the evening breeze, the Man and his Wife hid in the trees of the garden, hid from GOD.
>
> GOD called to the Man: "Where are you?"
>
> He said, "I heard you in the garden and I was afraid because I was naked. And I hid." (MSG)

What did God do? He went looking for them. He pursued them. Even though they failed him, he still went after them. And then look at what he did next:

> The LORD God made garments of skin for Adam and his wife and clothed them. (Genesis 3:21)

He didn't just pursue them. Once God found them, he clothed them. Though they deserved to die, God took care of them by making real clothes to replace their makeshift ones. I guess you could say God was the first tailor on earth. What God did for Adam and Eve has *everything* to do with what he wants to do in your life. One thing that we all have in common with Adam and Eve is that we're all sinners. God knows this. But regardless of your imperfections, God wants to capture you and clothe you by making you into the man he knows you can be, not a man who settles for an inferior substitute.

SEEING PAST THE SIN

Imagine how my daughter would feel if she ran off to hide and I didn't go after her. It'd probably break her heart, wouldn't it? But I'd never do that to her, because I love her. I'd never abandon her and treat her that way. The same is true with God.

After the first sin was committed, God knew what was in store. He knew that once sin entered time on earth, life would never be the same.

2 Sins + 2 People = Sin for All People

But an all-knowing God saw the bigger picture. He saw the potential in every one of us. Even though man's choice to sin broke God's heart and separated us from him, it didn't separate us from his love. God loved humankind so much that he was willing to allow life on earth to continue. Rather than destroy all people, he set into motion a plan that could bring us back to him. The Bible is the story of God's pursuit of us all. This pursuit brought God to earth in his Son, Jesus. Jesus's perfect life, death, and resurrection make it possible for us to be captured by God and forgiven of our sins, if we choose.

The day you were born into this sinful world and drew your first breath, God began his pursuit of you. He's pursuing you every day because he sees you for the man you can be—he sees past your sin to the real you. Sure, he knows you're not perfect. He knows you'll fail him sometimes. But he also knows that his plan for you is far greater than your ability to mess up that plan.

hit pause

Did you really let this info soak into your brain? If not, listen up. In spite of everything you've ever done wrong, God's still on your side. He's pursuing you. You're so important to him that in spite of the junk in your past, he has an awesome future for you. Just like the two naked runners in Genesis, you've probably failed God. And what does he think about that? He says, "I'm more interested in making you into the man I can use tomorrow than I am in the man you were yesterday."

You Don't Have to Run Anymore

Remember Barry's story a few pages back? I told him he didn't have to keep running. I told him that God knew about every choice he'd ever made and still loved him. I told Barry that even though he'd messed up in his past, God was still pursuing him and wanted a relationship with him. Barry stopped running that day, and he asked God to change his life.

Are you running? Maybe you are and you don't even know it—running from who you are, who you can be, or who you know God wants you to be. Eventually you'll run out of steam, out of breath, and out of places to hide. And then what'll you do?

The pursuit began in the Garden of Eden, and it continues to this day, in Barry's life and in yours.

To be captured, you must be willing to trust God. To fully trust him, you must first be honest with yourself.

hit pause

Can you remember a time when you've prayed a prayer and invited Jesus into your heart? Romans 10:13 says, "Everyone who calls on the name of the Lord will be saved." If you haven't, you can do that right now. Stop and pray this prayer:

Dear God,
I believe in you. I believe your Son Jesus died for me and came back to life. I want to give you my heart right now. Forgive me of all of my past mistakes, and take over my life. Right now I give my life to you. Amen.

If you just prayed this prayer, you've now made the most important decision of your life.

Just as God didn't turn his back on Adam and Eve and Barry, he won't turn his back on you. Even though he knew your potential to sin, God still created you. His love for you is so great, he was willing to take that gamble. Before you were even born, God saw you as the man you're becoming now. He wrote your life story before you even started living it. And now he's working every day to bring you into a close relationship with him. The question is not "Is he pursuing you?" The question is "Will you let him capture you?"

For God so loved the world that he gave his one and only Son, that whoever believes in him shall not perish but have eternal life. (John 3:16)

My Space

Write down why you're running. Be honest. Real change can never occur until there's real honesty.

Is there something in your life keeping you from accepting God's pursuit and giving him a chance? Write a prayer now asking God to show you if there's anything in your life keeping him from capturing you.

4

True Commitment . . . and Taco Bell

Want to know what you really believe? Watch what you do.

I met my wife, Amy, in college. I'm not someone who necessarily believes in love at first sight, but I must say that one look was all it took, because I was "diggin' that girl's chili"! (What? You don't say that?)

I remember the first time I asked her out on a date. I was so nervous. My question was simple: "Would you like to go out?" Her answer was simpler: "No." I remember being disappointed but not defeated. Because when it comes to girls, my motto has always been "If at first you don't succeed, just pester the snot out of them and eventually you can win them over." So I did just that. Every few months I would ask her out, and every few months she would say no. And this little game went on for about four years. Yes...*four years.* Finally she said yes. She likes to tell me that she felt sorry for me and finally gave me a chance. *I* like to believe that she finally got right with Jesus (ha-ha).

After more than three years of dating, I decided it was time to pop the question. I had a very romantic evening planned. I washed my car, put the ring in my pocket, and picked her up to go to this extremely hip restaurant in Nashville. You've probably heard of it—Taco Bell. Okay, I'm kidding (even though chalupas would be plenty romantic to me). After dinner, with the Nashville skyline in full view and a breeze blowing off the Cumberland River, I knelt on one knee and asked her to marry me. Fortunately, this time it didn't take her four years to say yes.

Consider this: During the wedding ceremony, the bride and groom each place a ring on the other's finger. These rings symbolize the joining of two as they become one in marriage. What if I took off my wedding ring and never wore it again? Would that necessarily mean I'm not devoted to my wife anymore? Of course not. The opposite is true too. Even if I wear my ring until the day I die, it wouldn't necessarily mean I'm a devoted husband. The thing that unites me to my wife isn't a piece of jewelry around my finger. It's *commitment.*

Think about that word *commitment* for a minute. What do you think it means to be committed to someone or something?

Here's what I think the word *commitment* means:

Believing in and choosing to live for someone or something.

This definition has a two-part requirement:

1. Belief
2. Choice

In my marriage to Amy, I believe in my relationship with her so much that I choose every day to live for it. This means that in moments of disagreement, frustration, or serious heartache, I'm still committed to my wife because I believe in us enough to live for our relationship regardless of the circumstances. The reason many relationships end and marriages deteriorate is that they didn't begin with a full commitment. There may've been a belief in the relationship. But there was never a consistent choice to live for it.

You must be wondering why I'm talking about marriage in a book for teenagers. No, I'm not advocating getting hitched before you graduate high school. (I may be from Tennessee, but I'm not that much of a redneck.) We've talked about seeing yourself the way God sees you. We've talked about letting him capture you. But there's another step: commitment. A good relationship between husband and wife requires commitment. And so does your relationship with God.

Andy, a high-school freshman in California, stopped me in the hall at his school after I'd just finished speaking to the entire student body. He said, "You're a Christian, aren't you?"

I said, "Why do you ask?"

"I could just tell by what you were saying that you probably believed in God."

"Yes, I'm a Christian. What about you?"

"I believe in God," Andy said.

"Okay, but that isn't what I asked. I asked if you're a Christian. Do you have a committed relationship with God?"

Andy looked puzzled. He said, "I'm not sure I know what you mean. I believe in God, but I'm not sure I have a *relationship* with him."

Andy's comments reflect a pretty popular way of thinking. There are lots of people who believe in God. You most likely consider yourself to be one of them. But believing in God doesn't necessarily mean you're committed to him. The Bible tells us that even Satan believes that God is real. But it's very clear that Satan doesn't live his life for God.

You believe that there is one God. Good! Even the demons believe that—and shudder. (James 2:19)

Believe It

Satan knows that if he can keep you from truly committing your life to God, then he'll be successful at stopping you from ever becoming the man God made you to be. How does he do this? It's simple. Satan strives every day to destroy your commitment by convincing you to believe things about God that aren't true.

think about it

What do you believe about God?

Commitment Begins with Believing

To clearly understand this, let's take one more look at the story of Adam and Eve in Genesis, and this time let's focus on Satan's role in the story.

> Now the serpent was more crafty than any of the wild animals the LORD God had made. He said to the woman, "Did God really say, 'You must not eat from any tree in the garden'?"
>
> The woman said to the serpent, "We may eat fruit from the trees in the garden, but God did say, 'You must not eat fruit from the tree that is in the middle of the garden, and you must not touch it, or you will die.' "
>
> "You will not surely die," the serpent said to the woman. "For God knows that when you eat of it your eyes will be opened, and you will be like God, knowing good and evil." (Genesis 3:1–5)

Satan, as the Bible says, is crafty. To be crafty is to "use cunning or trickery to deceive other people." The Bible's clear: Satan tricked Adam and Eve. Okay, let's call it what it is: Satan lied to them. Satan knew what God had just told them in Genesis 2:16–17: "You are free to eat from any tree in the garden; but you must not eat from the tree of the knowledge of good and evil, for when you eat of it you will surely die."

No Belief = No Commitment

Adam and Eve believed God. So Satan slithered into the garden and shook their belief system with a very convincing lie. He destroyed humankind's relationship with God by changing what they believed about God. Satan's the enemy, and he's really good at what he does.

Satan's lies continue to this day. Same song, second verse. He lies to you so you'll believe that:

- "God's plan for your life is a lie."
- "You don't need God."
- "You can do it on your own."
- "It's just sex. What's the big deal?"
- "You deserve to have everything you want."
- "Go ahead and take one look. No one'll know."
- "You're in love. Go ahead and sleep with her."
- "It's your life. Live it however you want."

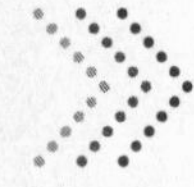

Duh, why didn't I think of that?

Satan's behind every bad thing that's ever happened on earth.

Behind every smell, there's a source.
Behind every untruth, there's a cover-up.
Behind every sin, there's an enemy.
Satan is the source, the cover-up, and the enemy.

Satan works hard to change what you believe about God. He knows your beliefs drive your choices and shape your convictions. He knows that if he can change what you believe about God, then it'll only be a matter of time before this change in what you believe will affect how you live. Obviously, this was the case with

Adam and Eve. I doubt they woke up on that particular morning in the Garden of Eden, went for a swim with the dolphins, rubbed their fingers through the mane of a lion, kicked back and drank some coconut milk, and then said, "Let's choose to disobey God today!"

Nope. Satan waited for the right moment, and then he moved in for the kill. He told the lie. Their belief system changed. This change affected their choices. And the rest is history.

You may be thinking, *How could Adam and Eve have been so stupid? They had everything they could ever want and need. All they had to do was not eat from this one tree, and they blew it!* It does seem pretty ridiculous, doesn't it? But don't we do the same thing? Don't we want what we're not supposed to have a lot of the time?

God says in Proverbs 3:5–6:

> With all your heart
> you must trust the LORD
> and not your own judgment.
> Always let him lead you,
> and he will clear the road
> for you to follow. (CEV)

When faced with questions like Adam and Eve, do you seek God's guidance first?

He also says in Galatians 6:7–8:

> Do not be deceived: God cannot be mocked. A man reaps what he sows. The one who sows to please his sinful

> nature, from that nature will reap destruction; the one who sows to please the Spirit, from the Spirit will reap eternal life.

But how many times have you checked out a picture of a naked girl on the Web? or lied to your parents so you could go somewhere they said you couldn't go? or drunk a little beer at a party? Those things just seem too good to pass up.

take action

Believe it by believing:

- God does have a plan for your life.
- You can be the man he wants you to be.
- You can stand strong in a moment of temptation.
- You're not a sitter.

The point is, you and I know right from wrong. Adam and Eve did too. But often, without even knowing it, we allow Satan to whisper lies convincing us that the thing we believe is right isn't always the thing we have to do. This is where the second part of the definition of commitment is critical—the *choice* to *live for* what you believe.

Choose It

The great divide between those who believe in God and those who are committed to him is one word: choice.

Commitment = Choosing to Live for What You Believe

In order to become the man God wants you to be, you have to not only believe in God but also choose to live for him. Making mistakes doesn't mean you're not committed to God. It's impossible for you to live a perfect life. But it's not impossible to live a committed life. However, that won't happen without *your active involvement.* This means you have a role to play. You, and only you, are responsible for your choices.

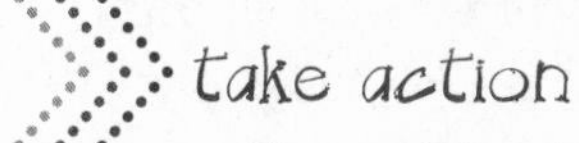

Choose it by choosing to:

- Spend more time in God's Word.
- Pray that God will shape you into a man of true integrity.
- Avoid hanging out with people who live against God's will.
- Get back up and try again after failing.

Unfortunately, Satan knows this too. After the lies have been sold, after your belief has changed, and after the sin is committed, you'd think Satan would be satisfied with his successes. But no. He then gets ready to deliver the knockout punch. Once you're down, Satan wants to keep you there. So once again, the lies begin to fly as Satan invites you into the "neverland":

- "Look what you've done now. God will *never* love you."
- "You'll *never* get it right. God will *never* use you."

- "God will *never* accept you."
- "God will *never* make you into the man he wants you to be."
- "You'll always be a sitter. God will *never* make you a stander."

And all too often, we *choose* to buy the lies again. We *choose* to believe that we'll never be good enough, never be godly enough, and never become the man God desires.

Is this where Satan has you right now? Just like Adam and Eve, have you bought the lie that God's way is the wrong way? Or because of something you've done wrong in your past, are you trembling under a fig tree, buying the lie that God could never really use you to do something great for him? If so, then you're choosing to allow God's work in you to be halted. You're choosing to let Satan use your past to hold you back and convince you that you can never experience a committed relationship with God.

Critical News!

You've got to understand why Satan works so hard to sell you lies. Satan knows the truth about you. We've already talked about how God sees the real you, but Satan sees who you are too. He sees your potential and your abilities. He knows God made you, and he knows God never makes a mistake. He clearly understands that you've been created for an incredible plan. And he's scared. More scared than a turkey in November. He's scared of the man you are and, more importantly, the man you'll become. He knows that if he can convince you to buy the lies, he can keep you from ever becoming the man God created you to be. And that'll keep you from influencing others to be followers of Christ too—which means Satan's killed lots of birds with one stone.

Live It

After trying unsuccessfully for almost four years to get Amy's attention, I could've chosen to give up. Instead, I chose to go get that girl and make her mine. Lucky for me, Amy fell and hit her head and developed amnesia. It was during her recovery that I told her we'd been dating for years. She believed me. And every day I wake up with the fear that today might be the day she recovers her memory.

Just kidding. I might've been desperate, but not *that* desperate. I made the choice to pursue Amy. And pursue her. And pursue her. Of course, God's the reason Amy and I are together now. But the point is, I didn't give up. I was active. I chose to keep going. Now, I'm not encouraging you to keep asking out a girl who shows you little to no interest. That might be considered stalking. But when it comes to your commitment to God, it might pay to be a little stalkerish. You've got to make the choice—and keep making it over and over again. You can believe the lies Satan whispers in your ear and give up. Or you can choose to continue on God's path and take him at his word when he says:

- "I've created you."
- "You're my mirror in your world."
- "You are good."

- "You're a man of responsibility."
- "I can make you a stander for me."

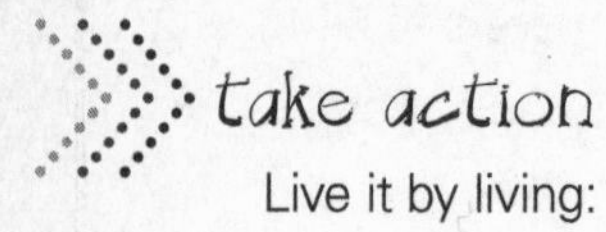

take action

Live it by living:

- one day at a time, striving to give God more of yourself each day
- to please God over pleasing a friend, a girlfriend, or yourself
- each day as if it were your last
- like everything you do can show God to your world

True commitment to God is all about believing in and choosing to live for him.

Not for the past. Not for where you've been or what you've done wrong. But for right now. For the future. For the man he made you to be.

My Space

Do you have a committed relationship with God?

If not, what's keeping you from being committed to him?

Write down five things you can begin to do to strengthen your commitment to God. Don't just do this halfway. Be really honest. Challenge yourself, and seriously evaluate your life.

Write a prayer to God asking him to give you the strength, boldness, confidence, and consistency to do whatever's necessary to create and maintain your commitment to him.

The Fall of a Rock Star

The good stuff in life is good. But what's best is better.

I always wanted to be a rock star. And I almost was…kind of. I remember one of the first times I sang a solo in front of a crowd. It was during the children's Christmas musical at the church where I grew up. Approximately one hundred kindergarteners through fifth graders were singing about Jesus, the manger, and Christmas bells. Everyone was dressed in red and green. All of our parents were there with cameras and camcorders. And then it was time for my solo, my moment in the spotlight. I guess it would've been really cute, except I wasn't in kindergarten, first, second, third, fourth, or even fifth grade. I was fifteen, and I was wearing a ridiculous-looking, bright red, full-body suit in the shape of a Christmas bell.

Okay, so it wasn't the most glamorous of moments. But something happened that night. Standing on a stage, all eyes on me, microphone in hand—I felt like I had found the thing I was created to do. From that moment on, practically all I thought about was music. All through the rest of high school, I took piano, drum, guitar, and voice lessons. I wrote my first song during my senior year of high school and sang it at our senior banquet.

Shortly after graduating, I moved to Nashville, Tennessee, to study music in college. Six years later I recorded my first CD. I still remember how it felt the first time I walked into a recording studio and actually heard one of my songs being played by the musicians hired to perform on the album.

Over the next six years, I lived the life of a musician. I hired a band. I had a booking agency securing my events. I recorded two more CDs and was making a living doing what I loved to do. I can still remember how incredible it felt to travel from city to city all over the country and hear my songs on the radio.

Everyone waits for their "big break." Mine finally came one night in Fort Myers, Florida. I was scheduled to play at a large youth event with several other bands. I was on right after a local band, which used a fog machine that filled the stage with a thick mist. It was the perfect concert environment: a packed house, an energetic crowd, and fog pouring off the stage into the audience, with lights piercing through it. I remember thinking this would be a night I'd never forget. Well, I was right about that. I ran out on stage, grabbed the microphone, and fell right off the edge of the stage into the crowd. (You guessed it. Thick fog.) This wasn't your average stage. This was six-feet-off-the-ground staging. Not only was I dislocated from my position on stage, but my shoulder was dislocated too.

I guess you could say I did my first stage dive that night.

Except when I dove—okay, *fell*—the crowd moved back, and I went *splat.* I climbed onto the airplane the following morning a sore and humbled man. I'm not sure what words adequately describe the change inside me during the following months, but I can tell you that I felt *different.* Not satisfied. Unfulfilled. Three CDs, radio airplay, countless concerts—everything I'd hoped for since taking the stage as an obnoxious-looking red Christmas bell was coming true. But I wasn't fulfilled. I guess you could say that "everything" wasn't everything I thought it would be.

I'm not saying playing music professionally isn't an awesome ride. It was a blast. But after many years of living the life I thought I wanted, I realized I was missing out on the life God had made me for. That was when I started to truly understand what it means to live a life committed to God.

Commitment: to Believe It and Live It

In the previous chapter we discussed commitment: believing in and choosing to live for something or someone. As a musician, I was committed. In college, I took all the right classes—music theory, ear training, studio performance, copyright law, and lots more. As a professional, I worked hard every day to get better at my craft. I couldn't have been any more committed than I was. But toward the end of my music career, I learned a critical lesson about commitment:

> *It doesn't matter what you're committed to if you're not committed to what matters.*

Believing in and choosing to live for something or someone sounds really good. But unless the thing you live for is truly worth living for, what's the point?

Let me explain. In being committed to a music career, I wasn't doing anything wrong. Actually, I was doing something good. I wasn't just writing and performing songs, I was writing and performing songs to encourage others to grow in their relationship with God. But even though what I was doing was "good," it wasn't the thing I was ultimately created to do. I was doing the so-called right things for my career. But I was missing out on the "best" for my life.

"Good things" by the world's standards:

good friends
good looks
good grades
good college
good degree
good job
good salary
good house
good car

The good things by the world's standards aren't always the best things by God's standards.

I'm confident there are lots of good-intentioned people doing good things for God while they're missing out on God's very best for them. Plenty of people settle for the good and miss out on his best because they've never stopped to ask God if what they think they should be doing is what he actually made them to do. After years of playing music, I finally came to the point of saying to God, "If you want me to walk away from music, I will." Was it easy? I can't say it was, but it felt right. Because when you do something you know is right, the right thing always has a way of easing the hurt over the thing you're letting go.

I came so they can have real and eternal life, more and better life than they ever dreamed of. (John 10:10, MSG)

Had you told me fifteen years ago that not only was I *not* going to play music for the rest of my life but that I would stand before more than two million people and challenge them about what it means to live a life committed to God, I would've thought you were crazy. Never in my wildest dreams did I ever think that God would use me to be a communicator and author.

My life as a musician was really good. But then God gave me an even better life than the one I dreamed I could have. But this didn't happen until I was ready to commit my life to what really mattered most—his plan.

God wants to do the same with you. It could be that right now you're not living for the "bad things" of this world. Maybe your deal is not an addiction to porn, smoking pot, hanging with the wrong crowd, or anything like that. It could be that you're striving to live a good life. But it may also be true that as you're aspiring toward what's good, you too are missing out on God's best because you haven't stopped to ask him what you should be doing.

A critical step for you as you become a man is moving from:

Living for the Good	• TO •	Experiencing the Best
Succeeding in life	•••••	Succeeding in your calling
Living for what matters to the world	•••••	Living for what matters to God
Drawing up your own plans	•••••	Embracing his plans
Seeing your dreams come true	•••••	Living beyond your wildest dreams
Using your potential for good	•••••	Exceeding your potential through him
Enjoying a good life	•••••	Experiencing the best life

God wants you to experience the best. Living committed to him, for what really matters, is the key to experiencing his best. As you allow him to make you into the man he wants you to be, you'll step closer to experiencing the very best he has for you. If you feel like you're ready to move from good to best, here are four critical steps for you to take:

1. Wave your white flag.

Commitment starts with surrender. Surrender is the first step toward experiencing the best life. Many people would have you believe that when you become a Christian, you have to sacrifice and let go of things important to you. Nothing could be further from the truth. It may seem that way at first. But really, you're not losing, sacrificing, or letting go of anything. What's actually happening is you're gaining everything—*everything* you were created to have.

think about it

Who made you?

Do you really believe that God made you?

If you do believe that God created you, then doesn't it make sense that the Person who created you probably knows what's best for you? And doesn't it equally make sense that if God created you and knows what's best for you, then fully surrendering your life to him will be the thing that makes you the most fulfilled?

Write down the goals you have for your life for the next five years.

If you could design your perfect future, what would it look like?

If God asked you to give up these plans and travel a different road than the one you're dreaming of, would you? Surrendering your life plans to God doesn't mean he'll call you to walk away from these plans. But he might. That's what he asked me to do—because he had something even better planned for me.

Waving the white flag of surrender in your life and letting God take complete control of your future is a critical step toward being committed to what really matters. A sign of being truly committed to God is being willing to walk away from the things closest to you if God asks you to.

Consider: are you willing to walk away from the most important thing in your life if that's what God wants?

2. Believe it—it's the real deal.

I met Alec while speaking at a music festival on the East Coast. He was one of the most focused fifteen-year-olds I've ever met. He talked to me about his future goals and his desire to do something more with his life than his father had done with his own. His positive, energetic demeanor turned more somber as he talked about a father who had abandoned him and his mom when Alec was eight. Even though he was still hurting over this loss, he was determined not to repeat his father's mistakes. Alec told me that he would one day be a great husband and father and would honor God with his life.

Alec had every right to be angry over a father who had failed him miserably. He could have chosen to sit on the sidelines of life, feeling abandoned and rejected. He could have fallen for the lie that his father's poor choices would continue in the choices of his own future. Instead, Alec chose to find the good in life. He chose to take God at his word.

Commitment to what matters means that you believe what God says—really believe it. Satan is an expert at selling you lies. We've already established this with the story of Adam and Eve. He wants you to believe that the past, whether it's your choices or those of someone close to you, will keep you from experiencing success in living out God's plan for your life.

But you shouldn't believe that. Every day you have to take God at his word and believe that what he says about your future is true. Check out Jeremiah 29:11:

> "For I know the plans I have for you," declares the LORD, "plans to prosper you and not to harm you, plans to give you hope and a future."

God doesn't say in Jeremiah that he has a plan for you *unless* you've blown it, does he? Nope. He doesn't say he wants to prosper you and not harm you *unless* you've made a mistake. And he doesn't say he only gives hope and a future to those who've lived perfect lives or come from squeaky-clean families. God says he has a plan for you—no matter what.

download

God has a plan for you.
This means that
no matter where you've been,
no matter what you've done,
no matter what your home life is like,
no matter what others think of you,
no matter what you think of yourself,
no matter what your past is like, and
no matter what's happening in the present,
God has a plan for you.

God has a plan for your life. He's customized a unique plan that only you can fit into. You're just beginning the journey of a lifetime—becoming the man God desires to make you into. As you grow older, God will be able to use every aspect of your life—the good, the bad, and the ugly—to make you into the man he wants you to be.

He's created you for this exact moment in history. And he wants to use you now to complete his plan. But you must believe it. Because what you choose to do with this moment will determine the *man* you become.

3. Be the "top dog."

I have a dog. Her name's Codie, and she's pretty special. She's part golden retriever and part chow. Yes, long hair and a purple tongue. My wife and I rescued her from sure death, or at least we like to think so—it makes the story sound more dramatic. We got her from the pound. She isn't the coolest-looking dog on the block, but I'm convinced she's the most obedient. I taught her to shake hands, not to leave our yard (and I didn't need an underground fence), and even to open the fridge and pour me a Coke. Okay, two out of three ain't bad. Anyway, she's almost twelve years old, which is like three thousand and something in human years. But after all this time, she still remembers the tricks I taught her, and she still obeys me.

Living committed to what matters will never be possible without living a life of obedience, because you can never fully become the man God created you to be until you're willing to obey him in *every* area of your life. You'll probably remember that a few chapters ago I told you that you're a man, not a dog. I said you shouldn't go around just doing whatever you want and only following your animal instincts. But dogs have some good qualities too—and obedience is one of them. So to redeem the dog population—and to help you see what God wants for you and from you—I give you this verse:

> GOD will lavish you with good things.... GOD will throw open the doors of his sky vaults and pour rain on your land on schedule and bless the work you take in hand. You will lend to many nations but you yourself won't have

> to take out a loan. GOD will make you the head, not the tail; you'll always be the top dog, never the bottom dog, as you obediently listen to and diligently keep the commands of GOD. (Deuteronomy 28:11–13, MSG)

What promises does God give in these verses?

- He'll lavish you with good things.
- He'll bless your work.
- He'll make you the top dog.

But what do these verses say is the key to such canine glory? Obedience.

God promises the very best to those who are obedient to him. Are you living a life of obedience? Don't rush past this question. It's one that deserves your complete honesty and consideration. Does your true loyalty lie with God, or are you just rolling over and playing dead? God knows the truth. He knows if your commitment is to him or to something else.

When God asked me to walk away from my dream of becoming the next big rock star, I didn't understand why he was calling me to leave the thing I loved. After years of dreaming, striving, planning, and working extremely hard, it didn't make any sense to me. But I did it.

Duh, why didn't I think of that?

Building an ark in the middle of the desert didn't make much sense to Noah.

David picking up pebbles out of a stream didn't make much sense to Goliath.

Jesus going to the cross didn't make much sense to the disciples.

Obedience isn't about what makes sense to you. It's about what makes sense to God.

I discovered that when God takes away something, he always replaces it with something better. Now I realize that even though I was letting go of something important to me, I was simultaneously grabbing hold of something much better from God. Sure, there were times when I questioned my choice to walk away from a music career. But I see clearly now that what I did was right. And today I'm experiencing God's very best because of my choice to obey him, even when it didn't make sense to me.

hit pause

Is there an area of your life you're keeping from God? If so, write it here:

Are you willing to let go of this area and trust God with it?

Write a prayer asking God to help you let go and give it to him.

4. Remove the headphones.

Imagine you had a friend who called you every night and kept you on the phone for two hours. Then imagine that this friend never let you get in a word during his rambling. He would go on and on about all his issues, never giving you a chance to respond, and then he'd just hang up. Or imagine if every time you logged in to your MySpace account, you couldn't respond to anyone who e-mailed you. What would eventually happen? You'd lose your relationships with these people because the communication would be totally one-sided.

Relationships are a two-way street—talking and listening. There are a lot of Christians who are really good at talking to God but stink to high heaven at listening to him. And most of the time the noise of their lives is so loud they never slow down, unplug the life pod, remove the headphones, and simply listen.

John 10:27 says, "My sheep listen to my voice; I know them, and they follow me."

There are tons of voices and noises competing for your listening ear. You have to filter out the noise if you want to hear God's voice.

How to listen to God

- Make an effort to spend time with him.
- After praying, sit quietly and listen.
- Slow down and give him a chance to get your attention.
- Take off your headphones.

God will never make you into the man you should be unless you're a man who's actively trying to listen to him. As you begin to train your ear to hear the voice of God, he'll speak into your heart his will and plan for your life. He'll begin to show you things you've never seen. He'll lead you in ways you may never have gone before. And he'll challenge you to think in ways you've never thought.

For many years, I prayed to God by going through my list of needs and desires. I'd be very sincere in my requests to him, but I was completely misunderstanding the most important part of prayer—listening.

No Way

Jeffrey, are you being serious? I've never heard God speak to me. I just don't think God speaks to people.

Don't be so quick to doubt. First, let me explain what I mean by "speaking." Most likely, God's voice won't boom from a burning bush like it did with Moses. He probably won't open up the sky, send down a dove, and leave a great message, as he did when Jesus was baptized. He's certainly never done that for me. But that doesn't mean he hasn't spoken to me. He's spoken to my heart.

Okay, that's just weird.

Yeah, I admit it sounds weird. But God is God—he doesn't have to just speak in a human voice. He has tons of ways of talking to us through his Spirit. He gives you that feeling inside that helps you make the right choices. (You know, the one you get in your stomach that says, "Don't do it. It's not right.") He warns you when you're tempted, and he sends messages through sermons, songs, and a million other things—if you're looking for them. He doesn't always speak out loud to us—even though he can anytime he wants. Just declaring stuff to us in his "God voice" wouldn't require anything from us. He wants us to really listen and pay attention, to train our ears, hearts, and minds to hear him, so he speaks in lots of different ways.

How God can speak to you

- in your thoughts
- through a song
- in the stillness of the moment
- through his Word
- through a friend

Do you listen to God when you pray? Or, just like I used to do, have you been guilty of running through your wish list of prayers, never stopping to hear what God wants to say to you in return? At the end of my music career, as I struggled with what mattered to me and what mattered most to him, I started listening to God. And I found out what I should really be doing with my life and what would really make me feel complete.

When you finish reading this chapter, take a few minutes to *communicate with* God. Notice I didn't say *pray to* him. There is a difference between praying to him and communicating with him. Start approaching your prayer life as a time when you communicate with, rather than pray to, God. As you get serious about communicating with God, he'll begin to reveal himself to you. And prayer will become more than something you do just when you need something, or at the dinner table, or before going to bed. It'll become a way of life for you.

Remember, the question isn't "Does God speak?" The question is "Do you listen?"

download

Pray to God: You do all the talking.
Communicate with God: You talk. He listens. He talks. You listen.

These four steps don't come easy. Living a life committed to what's important to God will take consistency on your part. Watching you live a truly committed life will make some people curious about God and what makes him worthy of all your devotion. And maybe they'll want to know more about him. But for this to happen, you have to keep doing the steps over and over until they become as much a part of your life as sleeping and eating. If you can start doing that, you won't have to settle for what's merely good. You'll be able to grab God's very best.

My Space

What's the one thing God is asking you to do with what you've read in this chapter?

If you don't have an answer to this question right now, take some time to get alone today and download this info into your heart. Then slow down, remove the headphones, and listen. You just might be surprised at what you hear.

Family Funk

Life at home can drive you crazy. Here's a plan to keep you sane.

What does the perfect home life look like to you?

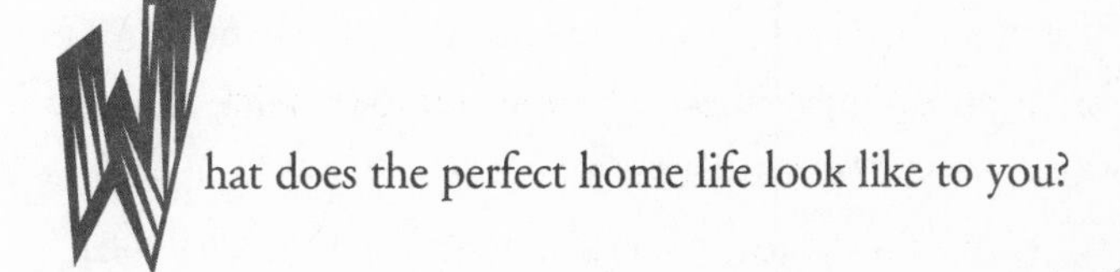

Did you write a description of what things are like in your house right now? I'll take a pretty safe gamble and guess you didn't. More often than not, people think things at home are way worse than they actually are. But if you really thought about it objectively, you'd probably have to admit your family isn't so bad. Most of the time, though, it's like you're wearing glasses with magnifying lenses: everything your parents and siblings do, no matter how small or benign, seems huge, like it's just another part of the conspiracy to ruin your life. And you're not crazy—someone really is out to screw up everything for you.

What you need to realize is it's not your family conspiring against you—it's Satan. This is the first of five chapters that focus on specific areas of your life where you might need some help living out God's plan. I'm highlighting these areas—family, friendships, dating, sex, and pornography/masturbation—because they're the parts of your life where Satan works hardest to get you to believe his lies. In your family life, his plan is to drive a wedge between you and your parents or siblings any and every way he can. And one of the best and most effective ways he does this is by convincing you that your family is worse than any other family. One after another, angry ideas will pop into your head, courtesy of the world's first and best liar:

"Your parents suck! Your friends' parents are so much cooler."

"Your parents just don't get you. Forget them. You don't need them."

"Your younger brother is so annoying. Just ignore him."

"Your parents like your sister more than they like you."

Family is very important to God. Why do you think he calls himself the Father and Jesus the Son? Why does he call us his children? Because he knows the bond between family members is one of the greatest and strongest this world can offer. So causing problems in your family doesn't just make you and your parents and siblings unhappy—it makes God unhappy too. Your job as a man is to make your family relationships better, not worse. So take a shot at putting aside the things that sometimes go wrong, and let me suggest a few ways you can make more go right in your house.

Getting Along with Good Ol' Mom and Dad

Whether you have one or both parents actively involved in your life, you probably drive each other crazy a lot of the time. Maintaining a healthy relationship with Mom and Dad is not solely your parents' job. Remember, you're a man of responsibility. Romans 12:18 says to "do your best to live at peace with everyone" (CEV).

Recently I was in Texas, speaking to students in public schools. One night during my trip I spoke to parents. That's where I met Pam, a single mother of three. Her husband had left her four years earlier. Her two sons and a daughter are teenagers. Pam explained how being a single mom and working a full-time job leaves little time for real communication with her three kids. She explained how her once close family was now falling apart because all of them were busy living their own lives and not paying much attention to one another. Pam was devastated by this.

I offered some possible solutions for Pam to try. However, in this situation, like many, it takes work from everyone involved. For healing to happen in many families in a funk, all family members have to do their part. Your number-one responsibility is to do *your* part—not tell your little brother what to do (even though he may really need it) and not blame every problem on your parents being "unfair" (even though their rules can seem really unnecessary sometimes). So how do you do your part? Here

are a few ideas about how to have a better relationship with your parents.

Honor Them

Okay, let's start with the verse I'm sure you've heard more times than you'd like to remember. Exodus 20:12 says, "Honor your father and your mother." There's no mistaking what God is saying in that verse. It doesn't say to honor them unless you disagree with them. It just says honor them. Period.

Children with good sense make their parents happy, but foolish children make them sad. (Proverbs 10:1, CEV)

Showing honor to your parents is easy on Christmas morning when they're giving you the newest video game system or, even better, keys to your first car. Respecting their wishes when you don't agree with them is a different thing entirely. In that situation, honoring them may not give you the result you're after. But consistently being respectful will show your parents that you're mature enough to obey them, even when it stinks. This will prove to be to your advantage someday. Take a look:

> Obey your father and your mother, and you will have a long and happy life. (Ephesians 6:2–3, CEV)

Plus, they might let you do more stuff if they see how respectful and mature you can be.

Be Honest

Think back to the last argument you had with your parents. What was it over? Does it even really matter today? If you're being honest, you'd probably admit that most disagreements you have with Mom and Dad begin over little things. But if you're not careful, these little things can start to become big things. When you and your parents disagree, it's important to be honest and on point at the beginning, so small disagreements don't turn into all-out war. When you don't communicate exactly how you feel, you build up a lot of anger and often end up saying something hurtful that you'll regret later.

But it can be risky to be open and honest, especially when you assume the thing you're going to say may not be received too well by your parents. That's why you need to remember these three tips when you're trying to resolve an argument:

1. *Always speak with respect.* Your parents may not agree with what you say. However, an honest word spoken with respect will get you a lot further than an honest word spoken with disrespect.
2. *Never speak with anger.* This may mean that when an argument starts, you need to take time to cool down before a discussion continues. Proverbs 15:1 says, "A kind answer soothes angry feelings, but harsh words stir them up" (CEV). If you really want to resolve a conflict rather than keep arguing, then don't forget this: Speaking out of anger will never resolve a conflict. It'll only make it worse.
3. *Choose your words wisely.* Speaking honestly is important. However, this doesn't mean that you have complete

freedom to babble on and on just to get your point across. Choose your words wisely. Proverbs 10:19 says, "You will say the wrong thing if you talk too much—so be sensible and watch what you say" (CEV).

Remember: Mom and Dad < Perfect

Parenting is a tough job. And your parents aren't perfect. No one could do what they do flawlessly all the time. But your mom and dad are doing their best, and their best is probably a lot better than you realize.

Have you ever stopped to consider how much your parents do for you? Without even realizing it, you most likely expect one or both of your parents to be a financial manager, housekeeper, personal shopper, launderer, chef, volunteer, medic, counselor, groundskeeper, chauffeur, and hander-outer of cash when you're in need of a financial fix. As if all that weren't enough, they also have more than just you to worry about: your siblings, your grandparents, their jobs, the bills, the dog you promised you would feed but never actually do…it's a long list. No parent could handle all this stuff perfectly, because no parent is perfect. And in case you've forgotten, you aren't perfect either.

So when your parents make you angry, try to remember all the things they do right rather than the few times they fall a little short. I'm sure you'd like them to do the same for you, especially when you're asking to stay out an hour past curfew.

Surprise Them

Anthony said the reality hit him during his senior year of high school: soon he wouldn't be living under the same roof as his parents anymore. In his effort to make the most of the time he had left at home with Mom and Dad, he blocked out time one night a week to hang with his parents. Going to a movie, watching a game, working in the yard, or just sitting and talking created lasting memories to take with him when he left for college.

When was the last time you did something special for a parent? Maintaining a healthy relationship with Mom and Dad isn't just about doing everything right in a moment of conflict. Be proactive in strengthening your relationship with your parents. I'm not saying to kiss up to them or angle for favors. But going the extra mile, especially when it's least expected, can do wonders for a relationship.

Surprise Mom and Dad this week:

- Clean up the house without being asked.
- Look around the yard for a project that your mom or dad hasn't found time to finish—and finish it.
- Take your younger brother or sister to the mall or to a friend's house to give Mom and Dad a night to themselves.
- Cook dinner for them.

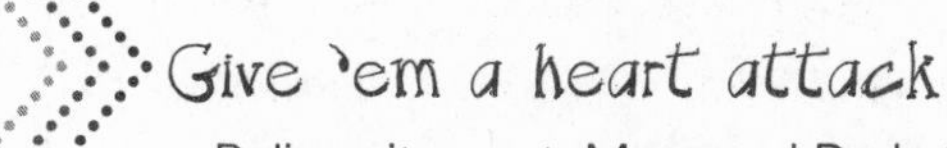

Believe it or not, Mom and Dad still like to spend time with you. Instead of hanging with your friends, take one night this weekend and ask your mom and dad out on a date. Take them to their favorite restaurant, and eat, talk, and get to know each other even more. And hope that your parents offer to pay.

Silencing Sibling Rivalry

I have two brothers. One older. One younger. Yes, I'm a middle child. And yes, this explains a lot about me. Growing up was never dull in our home. One bathroom, one go-cart, one Atari, and three boys always meant that someone was hoarding, someone was complaining, and someone was waiting in line.

I remember the time my older brother and I painted our neighbors' fence, without their permission. And then there was the time we walked across the top of a waterfall, barefoot, on incredibly slippery rocks, fifty feet above a riverbed. I also recall when we stripped down to our skivvies and water-skied past a boat full of fishermen. That was pretty funny, until I lost my balance and came to a sudden stop on my… Well, let's just say it hurt. We did some pretty stupid—and awesome—things growing up.

We had a lot of fun together, but like all siblings, my brothers and I didn't agree on everything. And a lot of times we found ourselves in some heated arguments, usually about really insignificant things like who got to hold the remote or whose turn it was to mow the lawn or who was going to ride shotgun. There were times when the arguments got really intense, and we would get so mad at each other we couldn't stand it.

But today my brothers are two of my closest friends. And the time I spent with Kent and Jeremy growing up made for memories that'll last a lifetime. The ups and downs of sibling relationships are a part of every family. And rivalries among siblings are a normal part of growing up. There'll be times in even the best relationships when conflicts flare up. But there's a right and a wrong way to handle them.

In the story about the first brothers on earth, Cain, Abel's brother, handled their sibling conflicts completely wrong. Let's see what we can learn from their story.

> Abel was a herdsman and Cain a farmer.
>
> Time passed. Cain brought an offering to GOD from the produce of his farm. Abel also brought an offering, but from the firstborn animals of his herd, choice cuts of meat. GOD liked Abel and his offering, but Cain and his offering didn't get his approval. Cain lost his temper and went into a sulk.
>
> GOD spoke to Cain: "Why this tantrum? Why the sulking? If you do well, won't you be accepted? And if you don't do well, sin is lying in wait for you, ready to pounce; it's out to get you, you've got to master it."
>
> Cain had words with his brother. They were out in the field; Cain came at Abel his brother and killed him.
>
> GOD said to Cain, "Where is Abel your brother?"
>
> He said, "How should I know? Am I his babysitter?"
>
> GOD said, "What have you done! The voice of your brother's blood is calling to me from the ground. From now on you'll get nothing but curses from this ground; you'll be driven from this ground that has opened its arms to receive the blood of your murdered brother. You'll farm this ground, but it will no longer give you its best. You'll be a homeless wanderer on Earth." (Genesis 4:2–12, MSG)

What a sad story. Cain made a terrible choice that cost him his brother, his family, and his future. As a man, you're responsible for being a brother who works toward unity, no matter the situation, no matter who's right, and no matter how wronged you may feel.

Love Trumps Pride

The story of Cain and Abel is the first story of many about two brothers caught up in competition. Cain realized that Abel had one-upped him before God. Instead of celebrating his younger brother's decision to honor God and commending him on a job well done, Cain allowed jealousy and pride to overtake him. The end result was devastating.

Proverbs 16:18 says, "First pride, then the crash—the bigger the ego, the harder the fall" (MSG). A real man understands that brotherly love always trumps pride. Work hard to be a brother who lifts up your siblings rather than tearing them down.

a little brotherly love

- Be a brother who defends a sibling when they're being criticized or made fun of.
- Keep a sibling accountable for their actions without being critical.
- A younger brother or sister may seem like they're always in the way. But remember, they most likely look up to you, and because of that, they want to be around you. Work to be someone who deserves their admiration.

You're on the Same Team

Family conflicts will never completely disappear. You won't always agree with your family members' choices, convictions, or lifestyles. You need to know that's okay. There's no one on this planet exactly like you, so there's no one you're going to agree with 100 percent of the time. But remember, God has given you your family. It's the only one you've got. So you should take good care of it.

Also keep in mind that in a moment of conflict, rather than fighting to the very end to win, no matter how angry you may be, you need to be a man who's willing to walk away. Cain wasn't willing to do this, and it cost him a brother and gained him a life of misery. Proverbs 10:12 says, "Hatred stirs up dissension, but love covers over all wrongs." Love can overcome any conflict. Strive to be a peacemaker in your house. In family life, disagreeing is inevitable. But as you're working to become the man God wants you to be, strive to be a brother and a son who promotes love, not anger.

Here are some suggestions to get you headed in the right direction.

Be a Slacker

The next time an argument begins to brew, regardless of whose fault you think it is, step back and take a breath. Most likely the thing that's got you upset will be long forgotten before you know it.

Also, if you're not fighting to be the one who makes his argument first, you will have the chance to listen to someone else. Lines of communication break down because everyone's more concerned about their own agendas than with actually trying to find common ground. More times than not, we fight because no one can button their lips long enough to listen.

You should be quick to listen and slow to speak or to get angry. (James 1:19, CEV)

It takes a real man to realize that arguing will never resolve a conflict. This is one of the few times in life when it's okay for you to be a slacker. When in a fight, rather than "fighting to the death," just cut them a little slack.

Check Out the Word

As you continue to grow and mature, you'll start developing your own convictions about your life. When you do, it's inevitable that sometimes your beliefs will be at odds with your parents' or siblings'. When that happens, you need to remember that God's Word never shifts or changes. When you disagree, the best place to look for resolution is the Bible. Turning to Scripture can be a powerful lesson for both you and the rest of your family.

Establish Rules

This one might really freak out your parents, but in a good way. Before you have another one of those wake-the-neighbors, call-in-the-reinforcements kind of arguments, approach your family about establishing a few guidelines all of you will follow the next time you find yourself in a family funk. I've really made this one easy for you. Below is a list of Cool Conversations Criteria that you can take to your parents. Read over it, add a few of your own if you want, and yes, you can copy them onto a different sheet of paper and really impress them with these ideas you came up with "all on your own."

ALERT!

If you haven't carried out such mature procedures in the past, you may want to ask your parents to sit down before you discuss these Cool Conversations Criteria with them. If they do happen to be standing when you present them with these criteria, allow time for them to get up off the floor before continuing the conversation. Also, be ready—there could be a momentary skip in their heart, loss of blood to their brain, or simply a shock that sends them into hysteria. Remain calm. This will pass.

Cool Conversations Criteria

In a moment of disagreement:

1. Give each person adequate time to talk.
2. When one person is talking, they must do so in a calm, reasonable tone. Otherwise, the conversation should stop until all parties have cooled off.
3. When one person is talking, the other(s) should listen without interrupting.
4. If the argument cannot be settled right then, agree to a time when all parties will reconvene to finish the conversation.

Manly Men Apologize

Have you ever said or done something you regretted later? If you haven't, then you just must not be very human. When you're willing to admit you're wrong, you show you're a man who's trying to live a godly life. Numbers 5:7 says a person "must confess the sin he has committed. He must make full restitution for his wrong."

Don't be a fool
and quickly lose your
temper—
be sensible and patient.
(Proverbs 29:11, CEV)

This verse doesn't say you only apologize to someone when you've been caught. It could be that, without their knowledge, you've wronged someone by disobeying them, lying to them, or keeping something from them. Your relationship with your parents and siblings will only be as strong as your willingness to maintain honesty. If you've wronged someone in your family, go to them and ask for their forgiveness.

Forgive the Funk

Everyone's family smells at one time or another. And I'm not only referring to when one family member has eaten a double pepperoni pizza. Sometimes family life isn't fun. Sometimes it's unfair. Many families suffer through divorce, abuse, addictions, anger, and abandonment.

Maybe your dad walked out on your family years ago. Or

your mom cheated on your dad and no longer lives at home. Maybe one of your parents hits you. It could be that your parents put you up for adoption when you were born, and you've never even met them. You may have a parent who's made it clear that they have no desire to be part of your life. These are really difficult things to handle, but you can always hold on to this promise:

> Even if my father and mother abandon me, the LORD cares for me. (Psalm 27:10, HCSB)

You may have plenty of valid reasons to feel hurt, upset, or even ticked off at a family member. And some problems are too big to be fixed simply by implementing my suggestions. But it may also be true that your anger, no matter how justifiable it seems, is keeping you from living a full, godly life. It may be holding you back.

You'll never have the answers to all the whys: Why did they leave me? Why didn't they want me? Why do they hurt me? There can be so many. You can't control what your parents have done or will do. But you can control how you choose to deal with it from this moment on.

Check out Colossians 3:13:

> Put up with each other, and forgive anyone who does you wrong, just as Christ has forgiven you. (CEV)

Listen, I know this one may not be easy. And if it seems like life has dealt you a bad hand thus far, I'm not going to tell you that you shouldn't be upset. However, you'll never become the man God desires if you're harboring anger in your heart. Do you need to forgive someone? If so, take a moment and write a letter of forgiveness to them. You might never show this to them. But releasing your anger can be freeing—even if you're only releasing it onto a piece of paper.

Dear ____,

If you're dealing with a painful situation at home, remember: your home life is no surprise to God. He knows exactly what you're going through. And don't forget: God never makes a mistake. He's placed you in the family you're in for a reason. It may seem like hell on earth to you right now, having to deal with your family issues. But don't give up—that's what Satan *wants* you to do. He worked to destroy planet earth's first family, and he'll work just as hard to destroy yours. Your situation may stink, but remember, everything is part of God's great plan for you.

Romans 8:28 says, "We know that God causes all things to work together for good to those who love God, to those who are called according to His purpose" (NASB).

God has created you for this moment in time. He will cause the story of your home life to help fulfill his plan for you. As God continues to mold you into the man he knows you can be, you can use the lessons learned through your family conflicts to help others through theirs.

My Space

Take a moment to consider your home life.

1. If there was one thing your family members would change about you if they could, what do you think it would be?

2. What can you do to become a better son to your parents?

3. What can you do to become a better brother to your siblings?

7

Friend or Fool

Who you hang with is
usually who you become.
(Are you okay with that?)

I knew I was being watched. As I was led through each security checkpoint, I felt more and more of my rights being stripped away. The prison was so cold, so quiet, so lonely that I could almost feel the heaviness of the concrete walls closing in on me. And I was only a visitor. I had always wondered what it was like on the inside of a maximum-security prison. I would never wonder again.

The building was fairly new and neatly kept. However, the evidence of a brutal reality showed on the faces of every inmate, revealing the knowledge that they would probably never see freedom again. When I met Jason, he was still a new kid on the block, in his first year of a life sentence without parole for murder. Jason was nineteen. We talked for a long time about his past, his broken home, a father who could care less about him, and how he grew up on the streets of Baltimore, dealing dope and packing heat before the end of fourth grade.

Jason could have made excuses for where he was. He could have laid blame for his poor choices on his family, his life in the inner city, or his deadbeat dad. Instead, he looked me square in the eye and said, “There’s no one to blame but me. I chose this path. I chose my friends. I hung out with the wrong crowd. Now I’m paying the price.”

Before he received his life sentence, Jason never stopped to ask himself if the people he hung out with were hurting him or helping him. He wanted so badly to be cool that he ignored his better judgment when his friends encouraged him to join a gang. He couldn’t say no when they pushed him to sell harder drugs. And by the time they got the idea to rob a convenience store, Jason’s character was so changed he hardly paused before he said he was in. He didn’t consider how wrong it was, he didn’t think about what could happen when they had loaded guns in their pockets, he didn’t think that someone could die and he could go to prison. But now he has a lifetime to consider all of it. And a lifetime to wish he had chosen better friends.

Friendships. We all have them. We all want them. And, to a certain extent, we all need them. Your friends are one of the most powerful influences in your life today. But do you ever really think about the friendships you have and how they affect you? Do you put a lot of consideration into choosing good, Christian friends, or do you simply search for acceptance from the most popular, the coolest, or the most exciting?

Who are your five closest friends?

Why are these people your friends? There are probably a lot of reasons:

1. They've accepted you.
2. You have a lot in common with them.
3. They make you feel secure.
4. You trust them.
5. They're loaded!

Okay, except for that last one, all of those are pretty valid reasons. But there's one criterion missing from the list: they need to live godly lives. As you're becoming a man, you need to think about whether *every* area of your life fully honors God. And your friendships are a huge part of your life. Your friends seriously impact you—how you dress, how you talk, how you act, who you date, what music you listen to, and even how you treat your parents.

I know you're probably thinking, *I don't let my friends influence me like that. I decide what I want to do. Just because I spend time with someone doesn't mean I always do what they do.*

Well, it may seem that way. But think about this:

Friends = Time

Friends are not just people you know. They're people you do *life* with. How much time do you spend with your closest friends?

You probably see your friends at school every day. You eat lunch together, play sports together, and maybe ride home together. Even if you don't attend the same school, you probably hang out together on weekends, work at the same job, attend church and parties together, chat online, text message, talk on the phone... It's safe to say you spend a lot of time doing stuff with them. Duh, right? That's what best friends do.

Time = Influence

The more time you spend with another person, the more you're influenced by them. That's natural. As you commit time to a friendship, your lifestyle will be more and more affected by theirs. Think about it: You probably like bands your friends introduced you to. And maybe you joined the football team because your friend was playing. Your friends do influence you a little, right? But why's that such a big deal? Well, think about this:

Influence = Character

First Corinthians 15:33 says, "Do not be misled: 'Bad company corrupts good character.'" How's your character? Do you find yourself making choices today that you wouldn't have made if not for your friends? If yes, have these choices been honoring or dishonoring to God?

Character = Choices

Make a list of the five choices you most regret making.

1.

Beside each of these regretted choices, write down where you were and who you were with. You were probably with a close friend when you made most, if not all, of these choices.

Friends = Time = Influence = Choices

God knows that friendships are important to you. And he wants you to have truly great ones. But he also knows how much bad friendships can hurt you. So how do you know the difference between good friends and bad ones? Well, unfortunately, your friends are not like bags of Doritos—they don't have labels on their backs listing all their ingredients. However, God has a lot to say to us in the Bible about friendships. In Proverbs 13:20, he gives us a piece of advice that can help in choosing the right kind of friends:

> He who walks with wise men will be wise,
> But the companion of fools will suffer harm. (NASB)

Read that verse again, and really think about what it's saying. There are two things I want you to make sure you see:

1. The Promise

The promise is simple: "He who walks with wise men will be wise."

What do you think it means to be *wise*?

download

A wise person: someone who knows the difference between right and wrong and chooses to do what's right.

If you hang out with wise friends, people who know right from wrong and choose right, you're going to get wise. Wise friends will be more able to offer you good advice in time of need, because they believe God's ways are right and they follow them. Simply put, wise friends will help make you a better person.

Do you feel like your friends are making you a better person in God's eyes?

2. The Warning

The warning in this verse is just as clear as the promise—and just as serious. Proverbs says if you hang out with fools, you'll become a fool. Right? No. It's even worse than that. Look: "but the companion of fools *will* suffer harm" (emphasis added).

If you hang out with fools, then bad stuff is going to happen to you. This verse doesn't say bad stuff "might happen" or that it "very well could happen." God's Word is completely clear. It says you "*will* suffer harm." So if you make the choice to hang out with fools, it's not a question of *if* you'll get hurt, but *when.*

Have you done things with your friends that have hurt you or gotten you in trouble?

download

A foolish person: someone who knows the difference between right and wrong and still chooses to do wrong.

Who, Not What

Notice that the focus of this verse is not on *what* you do. This passage of Scripture doesn't list a bunch of activities that lead to harm, like drinking and driving or cheating on a test or going too far with a girl. Even though all of those choices could lead to serious consequences, the scripture doesn't focus on the what. The focus is on the who—*who* you're with.

It can't get more direct than this. God's saying if you spend time with a fool, you'll suffer. That's why you have to choose friends who are wise by God's standards.

Fools have no desire to learn; they would much rather give their own opinion. (Proverbs 18:2, CEV)

If you're getting suggestions, support, and advice from friends who don't have God as a priority in their lives, then your life is most likely headed in the wrong direction. No friend on earth knows more than God, and if your friends start acting like they do know more, there'll be no mistaking which kind of friends they are.

Remember one of the Foundational Truths from chapter 1: if God said it, he means it. As you become a man, you have to be willing to accept God's Word as truth. If it's in the Bible, it's truth. So if you take God at his word, the reality is:

> If you have friends who haven't chosen to live lives that are pleasing to God, then you have fools for friends. And if you keep spending time with them, you'll have to suffer the consequences.

So here it is: are you hanging with the wise, or are you rubbing elbows with fools? If you're completely honest with yourself, the answer won't be too tough. But to help you in this moment of self-evaluation, consider these questions.

Do I have a friend who:

- consistently encourages me to do something that I know is against God's will?
- makes fun of me when I pray, read the Bible, or go to church?
- often lies about his whereabouts to friends or family members?
- encourages me to lie to my parents or disobey their wishes?

- encourages me to watch movies, listen to music, or view Web sites that my parents, my pastor, and maybe even I think are inappropriate?

God wants you to have awesome friendships. He wants you to have fun with good friends. But God also knows what can happen if you choose the wrong friends—which is why he's giving you such a serious warning.

Fools for Friends

So have you figured out if you have a fool for a friend? (If you have, you probably kind of knew it all along, right?) Facing the truth is an important first step. But really doing something about it is what separates the boys from the men. So what are you supposed to do? That's the question Derrick had when he wrote to me:

> Jeffrey,
>
> I have a friend who's starting to pull me down in my relationship with God. I know I probably shouldn't spend as much time with him as I am. He's not a Christian, and I want to spend time with him and help him see that he needs God. But I also know this can be dangerous to my relationship with God. What should I do?

Have you ever felt that way? If you've figured out your friend is foolish, you don't want to just drop him from your life without trying to help him. But pointing your friends to Jesus without embracing their lifestyles can be tricky. A lot of times they can end up influencing you more than you influence them. The important thing is to always remember what your goal is: helping them become Christians.

Throughout his life, Jesus frequently hung out with people who didn't always do right. But remember, Jesus knew exactly what he was there to do. He didn't just spend time with them to throw a party. He spent time with them for one reason: to show them he was the Savior of the world.

If you know you're in relationships that are not honoring God, you can still try to witness to your friends without spending so much time with them.

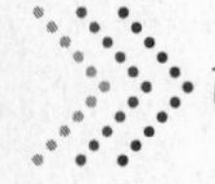

take a shot

If you're in a friendship that's not honoring God:

- Try to evaluate your intent for the friendship. Is your number-one goal to witness to this person?
- Cut back the amount of time you spend with this person.
- Be consistent in the life you live. How you live will speak much louder to this person than any words you can say.
- Pray that God will give you opportunities to share him with this person.
- Encourage this person to know more about God.
- Invite this person to church, summer camp, or a youth event.
- Don't give up on them.

Be a Good Friend

Finding and keeping healthy relationships that honor God isn't always easy. But it's an important step toward being the man God wants you to be. Strong relationships require a strong commitment. To find good friendships and make them last—and to avoid becoming the fool your friends don't want to be around—you need to remember the following.

1. Be true blue.

One sign of a true friend is loyalty. Anyone can be a good friend when everything's perfect. But it takes a real man to be a trustworthy friend who sticks around even when times are tough. Being someone who's faithful isn't always easy. Loyalty to your friends means that you:

- are willing to defend them
- are willing to overlook their faults
- are forgiving
- aren't going to talk about them behind their backs

2. Be honest.

True friendship = honesty. Sometimes, in order to be a good friend, you have to be willing to confront your friends about their unhealthy or un-Christlike behavior. Doing this can help them see their real selves

A friend loves at all times. (Proverbs 17:17)

by removing the masks that cover their true identities, their fears, or the ungodly lifestyle they may be embracing. A true friend is honest, even when it hurts.

3. Be a stander.

Romans 12:18 says, "If it is possible, as far as it depends on you, live at peace with everyone." A keyword in this verse is *if.* This word is proof that you can't control the choices of your friends. You can try to be a friend who encourages them to do the right things in life, but you can't control their responses. They may get angry with you. They may resent you. But encouraging them to follow Christ is one of those "if moments." You've got to do it, even if it disturbs the peace. Whether your friends choose to listen or not, you have to stand up for what's right. Be confident. Be true to who you are, even when your friends don't like it or don't approve of it. Be a friend who stands for what is good and right, even when others don't.

4. Be you.

A good friend will never require you to change to gain their acceptance. If you find you have to reinvent yourself to fit in or be accepted by someone, then you're probably not in a genuine friendship. A friend should never determine your choices. And if you let them do this, you're not doing your part to make the friendship the most it can be. Losing yourself in order to be accepted by someone else is never the right way to go. Plus, your friend won't gain anything from the friendship if you simply act like their clone. You should be sharing your best qualities with your friends rather than hiding them so you can fit in. If you've chosen your friends wisely, they'll like you as you are anyway. And they'll be hurt if you don't act like yourself around them.

5. Be a pusher.

Be a friend who pushes others toward a committed relationship with God. Challenge them to spend time with him by reading the Bible and praying. Encourage them to pursue God's plan for their lives so they can also become the people God wants them to be.

> As iron sharpens iron,
> so one man sharpens another. (Proverbs 27:17)

6. Be God's friend.

If you haven't figured this one out yet, wake up! Every topic discussed in this book *always* points back to God. The best way to be a good friend to others is to learn from the One who wrote the book on friendships. Just as your earthly friendships require time, you can't learn from God until you commit time to him. When it comes to being a good friend to others, your allegiance to God must come first.

Remember, life isn't about acquiring as many friends as you can. Proverbs 18:24 says, "A man of many companions may come to ruin, but there is a friend who sticks closer than a brother."

Rather than competing to be everybody's friend, be wise in choosing a few close friends you can do life with. Meaningful friendships don't always come easy. And there'll be times when distinguishing between healthy and unhealthy friendships will be hard. But as you commit to stay in consistent communication with God, he'll give you wisdom to know the difference.

My Space

Do your friends push you closer to God or pull you away?

Do you have friendships with fools? If so, what are you going to do about it?

What characteristics do you look for in a true friend?

Write a prayer asking God to bring you true friendships that honor him. Ask God to grant you wisdom to choose good friends and courage to walk away from those who'll separate you from him.

8

Don't Be a Dating Dork

With girls, things get complicated. Here's how to simplify.

All I do is think about her! I try to focus on other things, but I just keep thinking about her, and I really want to ask her out. I feel guilty because she's always on my mind. What am I supposed to do?"

When I read this e-mail, I understood exactly how this guy felt. Remember, I thought about Amy for almost four years before we ever got together. Whether you've been on a date or not, dating is probably something you think about—a lot. You can get so caught up in thinking about girls and relationships (and the possible bonuses of those relationships), about how much fun it's all going to be, that you forget dating actually requires tons of responsibility.

It's not the hardest thing in the world to let God into your family life or even into your relationships with friends. But inviting God into your dating life is a little different. It can also seem really inconvenient because a lot of the stuff you might want to do on a date isn't exactly what God would approve of. But if you want to become the man God created you to be, you need to remember that real men of God give him access to every area of their lives. And I mean *everything:*

- private life
- online life
- sex life
- partying life
- dating life

Yes, I said sex life. But this chapter is not going to be about sex. "What?" you say. "A chapter about dating with no sex talk?" Yep, you heard right. No sex. I've got a really good reason for this: dating should be about developing relationships, learning to share time with a girl, and preparing you for that time (way in the future) when you'll find someone you want to spend your life with. The point of dating is not making out or any of the other "perks" you've been taught to expect. It's about a *relationship,* and in a relationship you need to learn and do a lot of other things before you're ready for the perks.

Of course, you'd never know that if you took society's word for it. A lot of reality TV shows make dating look like a game or a joke. Just watch them for a few hours, and you'll take relationships about as seriously as you take Paris Hilton. And speaking of Paris Hilton, celebrities, whether in real life or on screen, do a lot to convince us that insanely attractive people run around having sex as soon as they meet someone, get married after a month of dating, and get divorced just as quickly. They *definitely* don't seem to take relationships seriously.

It's no wonder that when I talk to a lot of young guys, I discover that even the best-intentioned ones, trying their hardest to live God-honoring lives, are still completely clueless about what dating should really be like. The end result is that lots of them have taken a lot of wrong turns and made some big mistakes. What about you? Do you know how to do dating the right way—in a way that honors God?

God wants to be involved in your dating life, and if you don't let him, it's unlikely you'll ever really find satisfaction in dating. To become a man of God, honoring him in your dating life has to be a priority for you.

think about it

When it comes to your dating life:

- Do you ever feel guilty about the desires you have for a girl?
- Do you decide to get physical with a girl, then regret it later?
- Are you dating someone who's not a Christian and wondering if you should stay with her?
- Do you feel uncomfortable talking to your date about God or asking her to pray with you before you eat?
- In a moment of temptation, do you neglect to stop and ask, "What would Jesus do in this situation?"

If you said yes—or even maybe—to any of these questions, keep reading.

If you've started dating, you might think this chapter isn't for you. Well, you're wrong. You may have a lot of dating experience, but it might not be *good* experience. This chapter isn't designed to condemn you for anything you might have done on dates before but to help you have better, more God-honoring dates in the future.

If you haven't started dating yet, you might think you don't need to read this. Believe me, you do. You need to prepare yourself for what's coming, even if your parents don't let you date now (or if no girl's said yes yet). As you become a man, the choice will be yours: dating the world's way or God's way. I really hope that as you read this chapter, you'll examine your dating habits or desires and then apply the necessary changes as you let God make you into a man who honors him in your dating life.

hit pause

Some say Christian teens shouldn't date at all. I think dating can be a time for you to develop healthy, God-centered relationships with the opposite sex. Dating can cause a lot of problems if you choose to go it alone—without God. But approaching dating from God's perspective will help you develop dating habits that honor God (but still allow you to have fun).

Here are some dating dos that'll hopefully keep you from stumbling into any of the don'ts.

1. Realize that desire is okay.

Think about the most beautiful girl you can imagine—her hair, her lips, her curves. There's nothing wrong with desiring a girl. God created you with this desire so that you would find a companion to spend your life with. Take a look at Genesis 2:18, 21–23:

> GOD said, "It's not good for the Man to be alone; I'll make him a helper, a companion."…
>
> God put the Man into a deep sleep. As he slept he removed one of his ribs and replaced it with flesh. GOD then used the rib that he had taken from the Man to make Woman and presented her to the Man.
>
> The Man said,
>
> "Finally! Bone of my bone,
> flesh of my flesh!
> Name her Woman
> for she was made from Man." (MSG)

The Bible says that God created woman as a companion for man. So your desires for women are totally natural. God gave them to you. But having those desires doesn't mean you've got total freedom to fulfill them any way you want to—even though a lot of people will probably tell you otherwise. There'll also be people who say it's a sin to have desires for a woman *at all* and that you should try to kill those desires. They're wrong too. God understands the desires you have. And he doesn't just understand them. Believe it or not, he wants you to enjoy them. But with enjoyment comes responsibility on your part. Keep reading.

2. Know which girls are worth your time.

There's a question I get asked over and over again: is it okay to date a girl who's not a Christian?

My answer to this question is more questions:

Would you want to marry someone who doesn't believe there's a heaven, hell, or God, and doesn't believe that Jesus is their Savior?

Would you want to marry someone who wouldn't embrace reading the Bible, going to church, and praying?

Would you want to marry someone who wouldn't instill in your children godly character and the practices of praying, going to church, and reading the Bible?

I hope the answer to each of these questions would be a definite no from you. If this is the case, then why would you choose to date someone who wouldn't do these things? I'm not saying you have to think you're going to marry every girl you go out with (she might be a little freaked out if you talk about kids on the first date). But any girl you date should be marriage worthy. And the first question on the marriage-worthy test should always be: is she a Christian?

Look at what the Bible says in 2 Corinthians 6:14–16:

> Don't become partners with those who reject God. How can you make a partnership out of right and wrong? That's not partnership; that's war. Is light best friends with dark? Does Christ go strolling with the Devil? Do trust and mistrust hold hands? Who would think of setting up pagan idols in God's holy Temple? But that is exactly what we are, each of us a temple in whom God lives. (MSG)

This passage is saying that when you choose to unite with a nonbeliever, it's as if you're setting up a pagan idol in God's temple. That's pretty serious stuff. I mean, God warns us against making idols and worshiping other gods in the Ten Commandments. In this case, opposites do *not* attract.

But what if you could convince a girl to become a Christian after you start dating? I mean, if she really likes you, she'll want to go to church with you and stuff, right?

Dating a non-Christian may seem innocent. You may think that after a while you'll win her over or that it's just dating, not marriage, so it doesn't matter. But this passage warns that you're walking on dangerous ground when you choose to unite (even just for a few dates) with "those who reject God."

You may think you can turn her into a Christian, but it's more likely that she'll pull you away from Christ. People don't change just because you want them to. They only change if they want to. Talk to the girl about Christ. Invite her to your youth group. But don't even think about giving your heart to her until she gives her heart to God.

3. Don't avoid the bar.

Dear Jeffrey,

Where have all the good guys gone? It seems like every time I get into a relationship with a guy, it never fails that eventually he starts pushing me to do things with him—you know, sexual things. Why can't I just find a guy that accepts me and is willing to say no to the sex stuff? That's the kind of guy I want. Do you think there are really any left?

—Shelly

What Shelly was really saying in this letter is "I want a guy who will raise the bar. I want a guy who places God's desires and my desires before his own."

Most likely your future spouse is living somewhere on planet earth right now. It's possible you don't even know her. Remember, I didn't meet my wife until I was in college.

Since we've determined there's a strong possibility your future spouse is alive, it's also quite possible that right now she's dating someone other than you. What if you were able to call your wife-to-be's current boyfriend on the phone and talk to him before he picks up *your* future wife for their date? And what if you had sixty seconds to tell him how you expect him to treat her? What would you say? Most likely you'd give him an earful, wouldn't you?

You'd expect him to hold himself to a high standard on their date. You'd want him to raise the bar of excellence when it comes to how he treats her. You'd want him to keep his hands *off* of her. So let me ask you: Do you hold yourself to that same standard? Do you strive to raise the bar in how you treat a girl you date, who just might marry someone other than you?

the real deal

Raise the shades! Sound the horn! Wake the neighbors! In case you didn't know this, you know it now: it's a privilege to date a girl. Treat her like you know it's a privilege.

4. Respect and protect.

Several years ago, I was returning to Nashville after speaking at a youth event when my flight got delayed because of a horrific storm. My wife was home, alone and extremely pregnant. At the time, our house was being renovated. I arrived home in the middle of the night to find my wife sleeping like a log.

Things that make absolutely no sense at all:

Why do we use the expression, "Sleeping like a log"? I've never seen a log that was *awake.* Have you?

I climbed into bed and quickly fell asleep, only to be awakened several hours later by the sound of our house alarm. A door was not closed properly and had been blown open by the storm; thus the high-decibel, ear-piercing, send-your-cat-peeing-uncontrollably-in-the-dark noise. But my wife and I didn't know that, so we were a little scared.

We sat still in the dark, trying to listen above the scream of the security system to hear the footsteps of an intruder. I reached for the baseball bat that we keep under the bed for such an occasion. I'm not sure what good this would actually do for me, considering my batting average in Little League, but it makes me *feel* safer.

And then it hit me—*I'm tired. I've been traveling all week, and I know my wife is pregnant, but she's been* home *all week. And she's probably been in bed for four or five hours now, so she must be more alert than me.* Then I remembered how, during our wedding, the pastor had talked about how marriage required both of us to "give and take." The logical conclusion was to "give" the bat to her to "take."

Yeah, right. If I'd done that, she would've probably "taken" that bat and then "given" me a knock out of the park. If I'd made my very pregnant wife go look for an intruder, I would've been the biggest jerk known to man—*Guinness World Records* big. I was supposed to respect her, which means realizing that being pregnant is a lot tougher than waiting in an airport for a delayed flight. And I was supposed to protect her (and our unborn child) because she wasn't in the condition to protect herself. To be the man God made you to be, you need to respect and protect your date as well.

Think about it. More times than not, you're probably the one driving when you go on a date. So more times than not, you have control over how you drive, where you drive, and what you do. You should take this responsibility seriously and never put your date in an environment where something bad could happen to either of you.

Respect and protect by:

- never going to a party where there are drugs and alcohol
- never driving too fast or recklessly
- never parking somewhere alone where the two of you will be tempted to make a choice you'll regret later
- never taking her to a movie or other show you know the two of you shouldn't be watching

hit pause

Have you ever attended a party where there was drinking, drugs, or hooking up? So often guys say to me, "Well, I didn't know it would be that kind of party!" *Whatever.* You can be a man who rationalizes and makes excuses, or you can be a man who makes a difference. More times than not, you know what parties you should and shouldn't go to. Even if you and your date choose not to get involved in certain vices at those parties, the fact still remains that just attending a party like that makes your chances of getting into trouble about a million times higher.

5. Apply the WWJD approach.

No, contrary to popular belief, WWJD does not stand for "We Want Jeffrey Dean." (Well, maybe it's not a popular belief with everyone, but some people have said it... I mean, I'm sure *someone* has...) Unless you've been living in a cave for the past few years, you probably know that WWJD stands for "What would Jesus do?" The WWJD bracelets were once an extremely popular accessory, but today it isn't so fashionable. However, the WWJD acronym still represents an essential approach for you if you want to honor God in your dating life.

Do not be misled: "Bad company corrupts good character." (1 Corinthians 15:33)

"What would Jesus do?" Do you ever think about that question when deciding who to date or what to do on a date?

Wait a second. Jesus didn't go on dates.

Okay, it's true Jesus didn't go on dates. But he had plenty to say about staying pure and respecting other people and loving God before anything else—all important advice for dating, as well as life in general. So you may not be able to open up one of the gospels and read about a teenage Jesus holding hands with his girlfriend or anything, but you can learn a lot from him that'll apply to your dating life. Developing the habit of asking the WWJD question won't necessarily mean you'll always make the right dating decisions. But trying to approach the dating experience with the mind of Christ will keep you more focused on God's desires and less on yours.

6. Know that going solo isn't for losers.

I remember the first time I met Brad. Good grades, cool car, extremely athletic, and a good-looking dude. (Yes, I'm confident enough in my manhood to call another guy good-looking.) Brad was the kind of guy that every guy wanted to be and every girl wanted to date. But Brad told me he wasn't that concerned with dating at the moment. He said, "I can't wait to meet the girl I'll spend the rest of my life with. But until then, I'd rather skip all the hassle and temptation of dating. I'm having a blast playing ball, hanging with friends, and just being single."

Going solo is cool. You don't have to date just because you're a teenager and you feel like that's what you're supposed to do. In fact, choosing not to focus on girls frees you up to focus on:

- sports
- video games
- grades
- learning to play the trombone

- family
- college
- friends
- just enjoying yourself, without all the dating drama

And the most important thing of all: you'll have more time to develop your relationship with God. Girls will come and go, and maybe come and go again...and again. But your relationship with God is lifelong. And you never have to worry about him breaking up with you.

7. Cut Mom and Dad some slack.

Have your parents said you can't date yet? If so, you may not agree with them. Yet they're still your parents. And the Bible says, "Honor your father and your mother" (Exodus 20:12). (As if you've forgotten that verse.)

Instead of fighting with your parents, trying to convince them they're wrong, or going behind their backs and doing it anyway, why not try another approach: Obey them. Honor their wishes. Rather than defy them, work to prove to them that you're responsible and trustworthy.

I still remember double dating with my best friend Louis when I was fifteen. Louis and I and our dates rode in the backseat of his parents' car as they drove us to a movie and dinner. I'll admit that, at the time, this seemed like dating suicide. But now I realize that Louis's parents were just out to protect us. Going on several dates with Louis's parents helped me develop respect for the entire dating process. And once I started dating without a parent on board, I understood what a privilege it was to be given the trust of my parents—and to not be chauffeured around like a little kid.

You may not always agree with your parents' wishes. But keep in mind, your parents have your best interest at heart. If you feel strongly that you're ready to start dating, talk to your parents. Your willingness to discuss it with them respectfully and genuinely will show them you're taking responsibility as a man when it comes to dating God's way.

And when they let you date, follow through with that promise of responsibility. Only go where you say you're going. Only go out with girls your parents approve of. Come home by curfew. Call if you're going to be late. Don't ever give them a chance to regret letting you loose in the dating world.

8. Pray before your dates.

Prayer is a critical step to helping you establish and maintain healthy dating relationships that honor God. In Luke 22:40, Jesus challenged his disciples to "pray that you will not fall into temptation."

This one isn't for wimps. I'll admit that a lot of guys I talk to tell me they choose not to apply this to their dating life. Though it may not be a popular point, I think it's an essential one. Because prayer changes everything.

hit pause

Have you ever prayed with a girl before your date begins? Why or why not? Does the idea of doing that sound reasonable to you…or just plain crazy?

The next time you start dating a girl, gather up all your courage and try these three things:

1. Pray before picking her up.
2. At a restaurant, pray with her before eating.
3. As the relationship grows, let her know you pray for her and for your relationship with her.

As the relationship continues to mature, the hope is that she'll see prayer as an important part of your life. The ultimate goal might be that the two of you pray together before you pull out of her driveway. When you do, get ready. Because one of two things will most likely happen:

1. You'll freak her out, and she won't want to go on a date again. If this is her reaction, then most likely she's not the kind of girl you need to be dating. Better to find out now rather than five dates and two hundred dollars later.
2. She'll show her true colors, proving that she is, in fact, a girl who loves Jesus. And she just may dig you all the more for loving him too.

Praying with a girl on a date may not happen overnight. That's okay. Don't beat yourself up if this is a difficult step for you to take. Just continue to work toward the goal of being a man who prays with his date.

Praying before a date begins will:

- set the tone for the date
- establish a God-centered foundation not only for the date, but for the whole relationship
- send a powerful message to her that you want to honor God on your date

By the way, dating a Christian girl will make the praying thing a lot easier. Heck, if she's a Christian, she might even initiate the prayer. But the thing that'll make dating easiest (though not completely simple, because dating is *never* simple) is to let God guide you in every choice you make.

My Space

Make a list of the top characteristics you want your future spouse to have.

Will you hold yourself to the same standard you expect her to hold herself to? Will you strive to raise the bar in how you treat a girl you date who just might marry someone other than you?

Now, make a list of the godly character and qualities you'll exhibit in your dating life with other girls and, eventually, with the one you'll marry.

Make a pledge to yourself now to never compromise these principles. One compromise will eventually lead to another. Remember, no girl is worth the price of compromising your character, convictions, and desire to become the man God is making you into. Write a prayer asking God to help you and your future spouse stay true to these desires.

It's Just Sex, Right?

Before you go up in smoke, let's talk matches and gasoline.

In downtown Nashville, there's an adult bookstore (which, in case you're wondering, I've never been inside) with a large sign that reads: WHAT'S THE BIG DEAL? IT'S JUST SEX!

Contrary to the belief of this storeowner, and many others, sex is a huge deal. Whether you've been sexually active or not, you've probably at least thought about sex a time or two, or three, or four hundred. But before you turn a deaf ear to this chapter and assume you've heard everything about sex, think about this:

Remember how I said you'll never become the man God created you to be if you're not willing to surrender *every* area of your life to him? Remember how sex was on that list? Well, here it is, the chapter that tells you how to invite God into the part of your life that you'd least like to have him involved in. But believe me, it's probably also the part where you need him the most right now. Your feelings and thoughts about sex will get overwhelming.

(They may have already.) And the world around you won't be any help.

Countless magazine ads suggest that anything goes when it comes to you and girls. They even use sex to sell deodorants and razors, for goodness' sake. In beer commercials, women are just drool-worthy accessories meant to convince you that if you drink that brand of booze, hot women will appear out of thin air to fawn all over you. It seems stupid when you say it that way, but it works. It works because they're using the things we guys think about *all the time:* girls and sex.

Those thoughts are tough to handle—not just for you, but for everyone. Take a look:

> "We had been dating for two years when we finally had sex. Afterward we both regretted the choice. The relationship was never the same after that, and we broke up two months later." —Jason, 12th grade

> "I have never had sex. I have had the opportunity several times. But I want to save it for that one girl that I will marry. It is sometimes hard, but I am trying to do the right thing." —Seth, 11th grade

> "For me, sex is no big deal. I've had it before and will probably have it again the next time I am in a relationship." —Corey, 8th grade

> "I haven't gone all the way. Yeah, we've done other stuff, but nothing really bad." —Stephen, 11th grade

Thousands of the guys I've counseled have struggled with sex. Everyone has an opinion about it. And there's so much info flying around about what's right and what's wrong that it's hard to know what's what. Satan's doing all he can to deceive you into buying a plan other than God's. That's why you need to let God into your sex life. And that's why this chapter is a must for you.

Do you believe sex outside of marriage is wrong? Why or why not?

Do you believe that there's ever a time when it's okay to have sex outside of marriage? If yes, under what condition(s)?

hit pause

Sex can be an uncomfortable topic of conversation. So before we go any further, let's clear away all the awkwardness. Here we go. Every person (other than Adam and Eve) that's ever lived on planet earth has this one thing in common: we're all here because our parents did it. And before them, our grandparents did it. And before them our great-grandparents did it too (after the five hours it took to remove all those corsets and petticoats and stockings and pantaloons).

Okay. Once the words *great-grandparents* and *pantaloons* have been spoken in the same sentence, it can't get any weirder than that. So the rest of this chapter should be a breeze.

Sex Rocks!

God has created you as a sexual being. And he wants you to enjoy your sex life. I mean *really* enjoy it. Don't believe me? Take a look:

> Oh, how beautiful!
> Your eyes behind your veil are doves.
> Your hair like a flock of goats....
> Your lips are like a scarlet ribbon;
>   your mouth is lovely....
> Your two breasts are like two fawns....
> Your lips drop sweetness as the honeycomb, my bride;
>   milk and honey are under your tongue....
> Your stature is like that of the palm,
>   and your breasts like clusters of fruit.
> I said, "I will climb the palm tree;
>   I will take hold of its fruit."

Any idea who penned these lyrics? The author is King Solomon. Yes, the King Solomon in the Bible. Can you *believe* this is in the Bible? (See Song of Songs 4:1, 3, 5, 11; 7:7–8.) This is sexier than a Victoria's Secret catalog!

When I think of how beautiful my wife is, I'm not sure that "a flock of goats" comes to mind. But weird metaphors aside, this graphic description of two lovers is in the Bible for a reason: it tells us that God wants us to understand that sex is an awesome gift. And when we stick with his plan, sex rocks.

But God doesn't just reveal the sensual side of sex to us in the Bible. He knows that his great gift can be seriously misused. So he's also got some very clear advice for you about sex. Take a look at four words found in 1 Corinthians 6:18:

> Flee from sexual immorality.

Let's break down this verse into two parts.

1. "Flee from..."

Obviously you know what *flee from* means—get the heck outta Dodge as fast as you can. In this verse, God doesn't sugarcoat his intentions for your sex life. He doesn't say, "Stop and think about it" or "Rationalize and work to justify it" or "Just don't get too close to it." Nope. He gets right to the point and says, "Flee!" In other words, "Take off! Escape! Put on your running shoes, lace 'em up, and sprint full speed in the opposite direction!" It's clear that God doesn't want you to have anything to do with sexual immorality. But for many, this is where the trouble begins.

In today's culture, "whatever works for you" has become the new definition of morality. It makes it really hard to know just what you're supposed to flee from. The lines get blurred, and you can start making mistakes. That's why it's crucial for you to understand exactly what God's telling you to flee. Which leads us to the second part of this verse.

2. "...sexual immorality."

What do you think sexual immorality is?

Sex before marriage seems like the most obvious answer, right? But lots of people (maybe even some of your friends) think that as long as you just don't "go all the way," then everything else is okay.

Yes, in 1 Corinthians 6:18, God is saying, "Don't go all the way." But if you think that's *all* he's saying, then you're missing God's truest intentions for your sex life. When God says to flee from sexual immorality, he's not just saying, "Don't have sex before marriage." He's saying to run away from *any* sexual impurity.

> Among you there must not be even a hint of sexual immorality, or of any kind of impurity, or of greed, because these are improper for God's holy people. (Ephesians 5:3)

Sexual Immorality = Sexual Impurity

Satan wants you to be confused about God's plan for your sex life. He wants you to believe that the Bible hasn't clearly outlined what's okay and what's not when it comes to sex. He wants you to think there are all kinds of loopholes in God's rules that allow you to do some things that aren't technically "sex." But he's wrong. Dead wrong. God's Word is clear: impurity is off-limits.

Sexual immorality = Sexual impurity

Sexual impurity = Sin

No matter the situation

No matter the circumstances

No matter how in love you feel

No matter the emotion involved

No matter how long you've dated

And sexual impurity isn't just about actually being with a girl, doing stuff you shouldn't do. It's also about:

- your thoughts
- the jokes you tell
- the jokes you hear
- what you look at
- what you listen to

What does impurity mean to you?

Look at what Jesus said:

> You have heard that it was said, "Do not commit adultery." But I tell you that anyone who looks at a woman lustfully has already committed adultery with her in his heart. (Matthew 5:27–28)

That means your thoughts can be just as sinful as your actions.

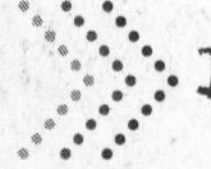

Duh, why didn't I think of that?

God says: "Flee from sexual immorality."

Which means: Run from all sexual impurity.

So what God is actually saying is: *Run to purity.*

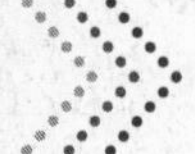

plan for purity

- Be wise about what situations you put yourself in.
- Have a plan of escape when tempted.
- Work toward open communication with your date or girlfriend about your desire for purity.
- Don't watch or look at anything that gets you thinking the wrong thoughts.
- When dropping her off after the date, don't sit for hours parked in the driveway, staring into her eyes...or her chest.

Know Your Edge

One of the most frequent questions teens ask me is "How far is too far?" Man to man, let me tell you—this is the wrong question to ask. Because when you ask that question, you're actually asking, "How far can I go without getting into trouble? How much can I get away with?"

Not long ago, I met this guy Matt, who's an awesome mountain-bike rider. He's been competing for years (and has made some serious money doing it). If you're into extreme sports, then you know mountain biking is about as extreme as it gets. Matt explained to me that in competition, bike trails often run near cliffs that have no guardrails to protect him from going off the edge if he makes a wrong turn. So what if he jumped on his bike, hit the trail, climbed the mountain, and then rode as close to the edge as he could without going off? Sounds pretty stupid, doesn't it? Of course it does. Matt told me that he always has to keep focused on knowing where the edge is. Even though Matt is an experienced rider, it would be foolish for him to see how close to the edge of the cliff he can ride before falling. Instead, he tries to stay as far from the edge as he can.

A man who's committed to becoming who God made him to be is someone who, rather than asking, "How close to the edge can I get?" asks, "How far away from the edge do I need to stay?"

Every guy is wired a little differently in this area:

- For some, all it takes to approach their edge is to simply look at a girl.
- For others, holding hands with a girl places them on their edge.
- And for many, it can be a kiss or a touch on the leg from a girl that puts them on the edge of trouble.

The keyword here is *purity.* Remember, God said to run to purity. You don't need me to draw a chart, list statistics, or walk you through the ABCs of living pure. Only you can determine when the line has been crossed from purity to impurity. Just like Matt, you need to know your edge. Know where this point is for you, and then make a commitment to yourself—and to God—to never approach it.

Any man can buy the lies that Satan sells. You know what they are. He's probably seduced you with them a time or two before:

"You deserve it. She's hot!"

"It's no big deal. It's only a little further than you went on your last date."

"It's not sex. It's just oral sex."

"Come on. Just this one time."

"What's the big deal? She's even willing to let you!"

As a man who wants to be made into God's likeness, you've got to man up and take responsibility for pursuing your own personal purity.

Switching Gears

Imagine if you jumped into a brand-new, five-speed Ford Mustang convertible—the ones with the new body style that looks a lot like the classic ones from the sixties—drove onto the interstate, shifted from first to second to third to fourth to fifth gear, and then all of a sudden, at the speed of sixty-plus miles an hour, decided to go from fifth gear to reverse. What do you think would happen?

You'd probably trade your car for an ambulance. Why? Because no matter how sweet that Mustang looks cruising down the interstate, it was never meant to go from fifth to reverse. The same is true with your body. Your body wasn't created to be able to get really physical with a girl and then just "throw it in reverse," draw the line, and stop.

When the physical stuff starts, it's very difficult to stop. There's nothing weird about that—it's how your body's wired. That's why you have to stay really far away from your edge. Because any time you choose to approach that edge, it'll be just a matter of time before you fall off the cliff.

hit pause

It's about purity, not virginity. There are a lot of physical acts that don't technically count as sex, but they are just as damaging to you spiritually, physically, and emotionally.

God Said So

There are plenty of reasons not to cross the purity line until you're married. I'll give you four:

- no guilt on your wedding night
- no comparisons to previous bed partners
- no unwanted pregnancy
- no worrying about diseases that leave ugly-looking sores, spots, and warts that appear in very private places

But the ultimate reason you should stay far away from your edge until your wedding night isn't because of consequences, guilt, fear of STDs, or the possibility of an unwanted pregnancy. Sure, all those things are extremely important reasons. However, the number one reason why you should say no to sex, and all things sex related, until marriage is *because God said so.*

Freedom

Since God is God, after all, he really doesn't have to have another reason for why you should do what he says. God said it. That's the end of it. But the cool thing is, God does have another reason:

If you choose the purity route until you're married, you'll find *freedom.* And whether you realize it or not, that's what you really want in life. Freedom is what we *all* want in life.

You've heard people say:

- "This is *your* life."
- "Live it for *you.*"
- "Live the way *you* want!"
- "Do what *you* want to do!"

Each of these statements has a common thread. Each is ultimately about freedom—freedom to live the way you want, freedom to find the very best in life, freedom to have what'll make you happiest.

The world says:

"Go ahead, indulge."
"You deserve it."
"She's beautiful."
"It's just one time."
"No one'll get hurt."
"Everyone is doing it."
"No strings attached."
"This is true freedom."

The irony is that the freedom the world claims to give you can only be found in Christ—it's what he promises. Lots of people think if they choose God's way, they're giving up the freedom to live the way they want. The world's way may make you feel free at first, but you'll soon find that it'll make you feel even more imprisoned than you did before. Just think for a second: When you do something wrong, you're weighed down by the fear that you'll get caught. Or you're stuck with some really un-fun consequences, like punishment from your parents, a failing grade, a wrecked car, a pregnant girlfriend... The list could go on forever.

And worst of all, pursuing the world's freedom takes you further away from *real* freedom. The freedom found in Christ is built on him—the best, the strongest, the eternal foundation—and it'll never leave you feeling trapped and empty. God's plan isn't about giving up freedom. God's plan is about being free. And Romans 6:16–18 makes it clear that if you choose to follow God's plan, you'll truly be free:

> Offer yourselves to sin, for instance, and it's your last free act. But offer yourselves to the ways of God and the freedom never quits. All your lives you've let sin tell you what to do. But thank God you've started listening to a new master, one whose commands set you free to live openly in *his* freedom! (MSG)

Are you in search of freedom from something?

Regrettable choices?

A failed relationship?

The past?

Guilt?

Sin?

You may think that true freedom can be found in sex. Oral sex. Hooking up. But look again at what God says in Romans. He says if you choose to embrace living this way, this will be "your last free act." The thing the world says will give you true freedom is actually the thing God says will destroy your freedom.

Freedom in God is:

- never relying on a sexual experience to feel fulfilled
- never waking up the next morning with regret
- never experiencing the emotional baggage, pain, or consequences sex outside marriage can bring

It's All About the Future Fun

One teen told me, "Jeffrey, one of the biggest reasons that I'm *not* into God is because he has too many rules I have to follow." That's how a lot of guys think when it comes to sex. They think that if they "follow God's rules," they forfeit the chance to enjoy "all the fun." Again, a lie from the great liar.

Before my daughter Bailey turned two, we bought her a baby pool. (No, I'm not getting off topic. Really. You'll see.) As you can imagine, she loved it. I remember one time she was swimming her little baby bottom off, and I needed to go into the office for a phone call, so I took her out of the pool. She threw one of those fits, something we always said our children would never do. Bailey was pretty upset because, just moments before, she was swimming and having a great time, and now she was being forced to go inside. To put it mildly, she was ticked. In her young mind, she thought I was trying to keep her from having fun. But as you know, I wasn't trying to keep her from having fun; I was trying to protect her. It's crazy to even consider that I would allow Bailey to swim alone. There could've been a huge tragedy waiting if I'd left her in the pool.

The same is true with God when it comes to your sex life. His plan is not designed to keep you from having fun; it's to protect your future fun inside of marriage. When it comes to sex—or any choice you make that's outside his will—he knows there'll be a tragedy waiting if you choose to "swim alone."

God knows what's best for you. He knows what'll keep you safe and secure. A sign of a real man is understanding that God's ways are best, even when they don't seem very fun right now.

Notice I didn't just say God's ways are *good.* I said they're *best.* Remember in chapter 5 we talked about letting go of the good in order to get God's best. The same applies to your sex life. It's easy to come up with some "good" reasons to do the stuff you want to do and then use those reasons to justify actions that are outside God's will.

"Good" reasons the world gives for having sex before marriage:

"I'm in love."

"We've planned ahead."

"I'm old enough now."

"It's prom night."

No matter how "good" your reasons are, if you're trying to justify something that's against God's will, you're trading his *best* for the world's *good.* Why would you want to trade down when God is offering you the absolute best there is?

ALERT!

God isn't in the business of just making sure that you have a *good* relationship with the person you happen to be dating this month. God wants you to have the *best.* Sometimes this is difficult to understand. But in order to have the best in your future, there are times when you must be willing to say no to what seems good in the present.

Ultimate Freedom

Look at what Chad wrote to me after hearing me speak at the summer camp his church attended:

> I had sex for the first time in seventh grade and have been sexually active in many relationships with girls since. For a long time I thought that because of my past, I couldn't change and honor God in future relationships. You helped me to see that even though I have done some terrible things, it's never too late to start over.

It's never too late for you to do the right thing. If you've made bad sexual choices, you can start over. Some call that secondary virginity; others call it getting revirginized. I call it ultimate freedom. Think of your life as a big Etch A Sketch. Remember the cool little red drawing board you played with as a kid? My little girl loves to play with hers. Personally, I was never very good at creating anything worth a second look. But the great thing about the Etch A Sketch is that when you mess up, no big deal. You shake it up, the screen goes clean, and you can start over again.

Your life is like an Etch A Sketch. And a good shake from God can wipe your screen clean and give you ultimate freedom. But to have it, you need these three things:

1. God

He knows where your edge is. Because he created you, only he holds the blueprints to your existence, and only he is equipped to help you handle this issue. First, if there's anything you regret, ask God to forgive you for the past. As we've discussed repeatedly throughout this book, one of Satan's greatest lies is to convince you that your past will keep you from ever becoming the man God wants you to be. But look at what the Bible says:

> If we confess our sins to God, he can always be trusted to forgive us and take our sins away. (1 John 1:9, CEV)

When we ask for forgiveness, he is ready and willing to give it. It could be that your past is the one thing keeping you from truly being made into the man he desires you to be.

Do you need to walk away from the past? Do you need your screen wiped clean? If so, write a prayer now asking God to clean up the mess of your past.

Once you've asked for forgiveness, you need to work every day to make God the priority in your life. As you do, you'll develop a love for him that'll burn stronger than any other love you might have.

2. The Word

Spending time in God's Word will change the way you think and act. Romans 12:2 says, "Don't be like the people of this world, but let God change the way you think. Then you will know how to do everything that is good and pleasing to him" (CEV). As you commit to spend time getting to know God, he'll equip you with the knowledge of "how to do everything that is good and pleasing to him."

3. You

As I said before, ultimately you're responsible for yourself. You've got to do your part. First, commit to pursue purity over impurity. One of the best ways to put this into practice is to establish boundaries in your dating life:

- Decide what type of girl you'll date, and never settle for less.
- Don't be a dating dork. You can't wait for the fire to get started before you find a way to put it out. Simply put: you can't wait until you're in a tempting or compromising situation to figure out what your plan of escape is.
- Let the girl you're dating know your expectations and intentions for the dating relationship. Be very clear about what type of parties you won't go to, movies you won't watch, and environments you won't step into.

- Be ready to say no.
- Be willing and ready to get out of any relationship that hinders your relationship with God.

Then remember that every day is a new day. The past is the past. You can't change where you've been, but you can control where you go.

My Space

Are you living on or over your edge?

If yes, what will you commit to do to change that?

If no, what will you keep doing to pursue purity rather than impurity?

After reading this chapter, what piece of advice will you apply to your life right now?

10

There's No Secret to Victoria

Every guy struggles with lust. But every guy doesn't have to lose.

I still remember the day clearly. It was a Friday afternoon during my seventh-grade year. As I'm sure the case is with you every Friday, I was excited about the end of another school week. On this particular Friday, I was even more excited because after school I was going home with my best friend, Steve.

His parents were still at work when the school bus dropped us off at his house. After we'd spent time checking out his horses, his new Atari, and his go-cart, Steve told me he had something else to show me. He took me to his parents' room, reached under their bed, and pulled out a box. Inside the box was a stack of *Playboy*s. I'd never seen a "girlie magazine." But I knew what was inside. For the next half hour, Steve and I gazed at images unlike anything I'd ever seen. I still remember wondering if Steve's parents knew that he knew about the magazines. I also remember not wanting to stop looking, even though I knew I should. I had no idea that thirty-minute experience as a seventh grader would still be burned into my memory all these years later. But it is. I don't remember much about the seventh grade, but I still remember those pictures. I can also still remember how ashamed and guilty I felt afterward.

> You have heard that it was said, "Do not commit adultery." But I tell you that anyone who looks at a woman lustfully has already committed adultery with her in his heart. (Matthew 5:27–28)

You probably remember that verse from the last chapter. And you probably remember that Jesus said it. The woman he's talking about doesn't have to be a live woman—she can be in a picture, in a video, or on your computer screen. I felt guilt and shame that day in seventh grade because I had a serious encounter with lust (and with simply doing what I knew I shouldn't). Lust is powerful—and dangerous. Lust is why *Playboy* exists.

But these days you don't have to look under any beds to find lust-worthy stuff. It's everywhere. You can see about as much skin as I saw that day just by flipping through *Maxim* or walking past Abercrombie & Fitch or Victoria's Secret. (By the way, have you ever wondered why the name is Victoria's Secret? It's definitely no secret what "Victoria" is all about.) Billboards, commercials, music videos—you don't have to look far to find stuff that's just barely this side of pornographic. And then of course you've got the real stuff—the magazines and movies and Internet sites that are completely, 100 percent pornographic. But whether it's the stuff anyone can get their hands on or the contraband you have to be eighteen to buy, all of it can knock you off the path God wants you to be on.

By definition, the word *pornography* isn't only about nudity. It's about causing sexual arousal. It's about making you have feelings and do things that should be shared with your future wife. You may think you're "just looking," but those images are setting off lust explosions in your brain. And many times that leads to something you'd probably rather not discuss—masturbation.

download

por-nog-ra-phy (n.) –sexually explicit pictures, writing, or other material whose primary purpose is to cause sexual arousal; the presentation or production of this material.

There've been countless books, blogs, and articles written about whether or not masturbation is wrong. Rather than asking if the act is right or wrong, the more important question is, "Is it pure?" I've never talked to a guy your age struggling with masturbation who said he didn't also fantasize about a girl while doing it. I'm pretty sure you also know that lustful thoughts and masturbation are not sold separately. And since fantasizing and lusting are impure acts—sin—then masturbation is stamped with the same label.

Acting out your lust may seem satisfying in the moment. And these days, guys joke with each other about stealing their sisters' magazines and using them as "inspiration," like it's no big deal. Masturbation and teen boys seem to go hand in hand—we think that's simply what guys that age do. But don't fool yourself. The purity we talked about in the last chapter isn't just about keeping your hands off girls. It's about trying to keep your mind off them too. Because, if you're not careful, lust will prevent you from becoming the man God is making you to be.

The Lust Fallacy

- That it satisfies.
- That it gives you a glimpse of what sex will be like in marriage.
- That it fulfills sexual fantasies.

The Lust Reality

1. Lust can't be avoided.

Be self-controlled and alert. Your enemy the devil prowls around like a roaring lion looking for someone to devour. (1 Peter 5:8)

Reese was an eighteen-year-old counselor at a camp where I spoke one summer. He was an exceptional leader and a great role model to the campers, and he could play a mean guitar. During the two weeks at camp, I spent a lot of time with Reese and was impressed by him in a lot of ways. One night, during worship, Reese asked me to pray for him. He admitted he had an addiction to porn. He'd accidentally stumbled upon a porn site on the Internet, and one look was all it took to get him hooked. Reese was a great guy who was striving to live for Jesus, but he'd made a costly mistake.

Many guys I've counseled who are controlled by their lust, or even the ones who just slip up occasionally, didn't initially go searching for pictures of naked girls or whatever else turned them on. That stuff found them. At some point, it'll find you too. The question is, will you be prepared to handle it?

2. Lust never satisfies.

Since the first sin in the Garden of Eden, taking a bite of the "fresh and delicious" has been tempting. But the problem with lust is it never satisfies the hunger. It'll always leave you wanting more, and more, and more. And what may initially seem like an innocent bite can quickly turn into a harmful habit or a dark addiction.

3. Lust infects your mind's hard drive.

"The hardest part about not looking at porn anymore is the pictures in my mind. I can still see those pictures!" When I read this e-mail from Chad, I knew exactly what he meant. When you look at porn—or any kind of sexually arousing stuff—you're actually downloading images into your mind's hard drive that will be extremely difficult to delete. That's why just one look can be so dangerous. You may only look at those pictures one time, but they'll stay with you—and continue to tempt you—for much, much longer.

4. Lust blinds you.

The more time you spend "taking care of your own needs," the more your view of girls will change. Eventually, you won't be able to see girls as God sees them. Instead they'll just be objects there to fulfill your desires. And the more distorted your view of girls gets, the less respect you'll have for them. A disrespectful guy who treats girls like objects may be the norm in the media these days, but those aren't the qualities that win over nice girls. And they're definitely not the qualities God created you to have.

5. Lust encourages you to give life to your cybergirl.

Looking at a cybergirl, and maybe doing more than just looking at her, will eventually become old school. When the online fantasy no longer satisfies, that fantasy will fight to make itself reality by enticing you to bring the pornographic images to life with a *real* girl.

6. Lust destroys relationships.

Porn and masturbation will create a fantasy world in your mind that just can't exist in the real world. It's impossible. Those things are clearly aimed at satisfying your own selfish desires. In reality, relationships take two, but in your lust-driven fantasy, it's all about you. The more time you spend in your alternate reality, the more you'll destroy the basic character traits needed in any healthy relationship, like sharing, trust, honesty, and faithfulness. If you don't develop these characteristics, your selfishness will keep you from finding the happiness God wants for you.

7. Lust destroys your character.

As you dive deeper into the world of self-gratification, your character will be destroyed. Galatians 6:7–8 says, "A man reaps what he sows. The one who sows to please his sinful nature, from that nature will reap destruction." You're really being fooled if you think you can casually dabble in porn and masturbation and also live the life God would have you live. We've talked a lot about showing God to people when they're watching. But you should also be God's mirror even when no one's watching. If you don't, your character will become more worldly than godly. Make no mistake, if you let Satan into one part of your life, pretty soon he'll be on his way to taking over all of it.

the Truth

Above all else, guard your heart,
for it is the wellspring of life....
Let your eyes look straight ahead,
fix your gaze directly before you.
Make level paths for your feet
and take only ways that are firm.
Do not swerve to the right or the left;
keep your foot from evil.
(Proverbs 4:23, 25–27)

If you're struggling with lust, you're not alone. And if it's not a problem for you right now, you need to make sure it'll never be. Every man, at some point in his life, will have to fight incredibly hard against sexual temptation. The ones who overcome it are the ones who are man enough to first admit that they have a problem and then get serious about defeating it.

So the choice is yours. What will you do when temptation overtakes you? Will you:

- choose to do nothing?
- assume it'll never find you?
- think it's no big deal?
- sit idly and hope for the best?

Guarding your heart is a big responsibility. You have to be proactive. Here are some suggestions that will help you win the struggle with lust, now… and later.

1. Make a choice.

Choosing a life of purity is the first step. You've got to decide that you don't want to live under the guilt that lust creates and choose to get serious about defeating it.

2. Protect your mind's eye.

The struggle with lust doesn't begin in your pants. It begins in your mind. Don't look at porn or read magazines, listen to music, or watch any TV show

the Truth

So let God work his will in you. Yell a loud *no* to the Devil and watch him scamper. Say a quiet *yes* to God and he'll be there in no time. Quit dabbling in sin. Purify your inner life. Quit playing the field. Hit bottom, and cry your eyes out. The fun and games are over. Get serious, really serious. Get down on your knees before the Master; it's the only way you'll get on your feet. (James 4:7–10, MSG)

that might send impure thoughts racing through your brain.

But let God change the way you think. Then you will know how to do everything that is good and pleasing to him. (Romans 12:2, CEV)

3. Know what you can't do.

We've talked about knowing your edge when it comes to sex. The same goes for lust. Different people have different things that flip that "dirty" switch in their minds. Maybe using the Internet late at night while your parents are asleep tempts you to just glance at a Web site you shouldn't. Or it could be something a lot simpler, like watching a movie or thinking about a girl at school you really like. Or even something that seems sort of dumb when you think about it, like staying in the shower too long or looking at a girl's feet (don't worry, I won't tell anyone about your foot fetish). Only you know what gets you going, and only you know where to draw the line.

Make a list of all the things that tempt you, and then be determined to avoid these things:

4. Know your way out.

Have a plan of action that you'll use when you're tempted. Again, winning the war with porn and masturbation is all about winning the war in your mind. The key is to get your mind on something else.

Look back at your list of temptations from number 3. What will be your way out if you're confronted with any of them?

A guy I counseled told me what helped him get his mind off his lustful thoughts:

> I used to feel tempted to look at porn at night in my bedroom when I used the Internet. So I started watching TV in my bed at night rather than getting online. TV took my mind off of it and helped me avoid feeling tempted.

Here are some other escape tactics you might use:

- Turn on the radio to get your mind off what you know you shouldn't do.

- Wear a bunch of layers of clothes to bed. Yeah, this sounds really silly. But think about it—when tempted, if you have to remove four different layers of pants, by the time you take them all off, you'll have had time to stop and think about what you're doing and hopefully talk yourself out of it.
- If you're in bed thinking some impure thoughts about that girl in algebra class, get out of bed and turn on the lights.
- Go for a run.
- Call a friend.
- Open your Bible and read a chapter or two.
- Give the dog a bath. (Hey, if that doesn't put you completely out of the mood, I don't know what will.)

5. Arm yourself with Scripture.

I know you're probably thinking, *Sure, Jeffrey…I'm going to actually recite a verse while I'm thinking about masturbating!* It may sound ludicrous. But check out Psalm 119:9, 11: "Young people can live a clean life by obeying your word.… I treasure your word above all else; it keeps me from sinning against you" (CEV). Find a scripture that works for you, memorize it, and repeat it out loud whenever you feel tempted.

6. Set a goal.

Set a realistic goal that you can work toward. For instance, try not to masturbate or look at porn for one week. After reaching the goal, reward yourself with your favorite meal, a movie, or an iTunes purchase. Then go for two weeks, a month, two months. After you make it to your early, shorter goals, the longer ones will seem a little easier to reach.

Christ gives me the strength to face anything. (Philippians 4:13, CEV)

7. Strive for purity.

If you want to become a man more in tune with God, you can't do it if you're consistently focusing on an impure thought. Whether it's masturbation, lying, or cheating, you should want to strive to be a man of purity who honors God in *every* area of his life.

Each one is tempted when, by his own evil desire, he is dragged away and enticed. Then, after desire has conceived, it gives birth to sin; and sin, when it is full-grown, gives birth to death. (James 1:14–15)

hit pause

Pray that God will give you the desire to become a man of purity, not just on the outside, but in your heart and mind too. When you do fail, ask God to give you strength to move forward rather than looking back.

8. Hold yourself accountable.

I made a covenant with my eyes not to look lustfully at a girl. (Job 31:1)

If you've got a problem with lust, you probably feel guilty, embarrassed, and maybe even helpless. But remember, you're not alone. Every guy will fight against lust of one form or another. Rather than making excuses like a lot of people do, choose to take action. One way to do this is to find a friend or adult you can talk to openly about your feelings, frustrations, temptations, and setbacks.

One teen recently wrote me that he had put this step to practice. He said, "I found an accountability partner, just like you suggested during your message. At first I was nervous about sharing my personal stuff with someone. But it felt so good just to come clean with a friend who understands what I'm going through. We really have become close through it all and now hold each other to the fire when it comes to girls, porn, and all the physical temptations."

You can do this too. As you strive to make a commitment like the one in Job 31, share it with someone you trust who'll hold you accountable by asking you the tough questions about your private life. Commit to check in with this person consistently. Also, spend time praying together.

The proof is in the verse: you must do your part in the fight against lust.

9. Don't give up.

> We must get rid of everything that slows us down, especially the sin that just won't let go. And we must be determined to run the race that is ahead of us. We must keep our eyes on Jesus, who leads us and makes our faith complete. (Hebrews 12:1–2, CEV)

If you're struggling with lust, the problem didn't just appear overnight, and you most likely won't get rid of it overnight either. Work hard every day to do these steps I've given you. But don't kick yourself when you give in to temptation. Remember, the race you're running isn't a hundred-yard dash—it's a marathon. There'll be times when you fail. But don't use this as an excuse to give up. Rather, use it as a reminder that you've got to rely on God to help you overcome this or any other problem you have.

My Space

If you're like most guys, you've probably given in to your temptations a lot and then prayed to ask God to forgive you, only to find yourself days later, or maybe even hours later, repeating the same mistakes. Don't give up. God hasn't given up on you. So don't give up on yourself.

> If we confess our sins, he is faithful and just and will forgive us our sins and purify us from all unrighteousness. (1 John 1:9)

If you're getting hooked on porn, confess, and give this problem to God.

1. Ask for forgiveness from God.
2. Ask God to give you courage to apply the steps in this chapter.
3. Write out a contract with yourself that says you'll stop doing what you're doing.
4. Keep the contract in a place where it'll remind you of your commitment.
5. Commit this contract to God.

Contract with Myself

I've given you a lot of suggestions in this chapter. Don't let it overwhelm you. Instead, focus on one step you'll really work to implement today. And then, in time, try to apply other steps as well.

What one step will I apply to my life today?

Go to Hell

The problem with saying nothing is what your silence says. (It's a lot more than you think.)

Locker 121. I still remember my junior-high locker number all these years later. As much time as I spent inside it, there's really no way I could forget. It's not as bad as you'd imagine—being in a locker, I mean—especially if it's before lunch and you're stuck in there with a PB & J sandwich and a Dew.

I didn't go in my locker of my own free will. I was forced in by several punks in my school. And the ringleader of the punkheads was a guy named Eric. Eric and I were enemies. He used to sit behind me in algebra class and thump me on the back of the head. And to this day, if someone pops me upside the head, it quickly brings back memories of 9:00 a.m. algebra, Eric, and headaches.

I often wondered why Eric didn't like me. That is, until the day he told me it was because I was a Christian. All through junior high and high school, it seemed Eric's goal in life, other than acting like a complete "donkey," was to totally ruin six years of my existence. Therefore, you can imagine, when I heard God tell me that he wanted me to talk to Eric about what it meant to be a Christian, I assumed God was mistaken. I remember laughing at first. But he wasn't joking. God really wanted me to talk about him with Eric.

I intentionally ignored his request for four months. And I was miserable because of it. I knew what God wanted me to do. And I knew I would stay miserable until I did it. So finally I called Eric on the phone, in part because I really enjoyed my nose and didn't want to lose it if Eric decided to take a swing at it. Having prepared my thoughts long before I made the call, I must say, I gave the speech of my life. And to my surprise, Eric listened. Giving myself a big high-five for a job well done, I then finished by asking if Eric would like to pray to receive Jesus into his life. Eric politely said no. And he hung up the phone.

What? You have got to be kidding, I thought. It wasn't supposed to work this way. I remember praying to God and saying, *I did what you asked me to, and you didn't come through for me! I put my neck on the line with a guy I can't even stand to look at, and it didn't work!* I was mad. Mad at God.

hit pause

Is there someone in your life who doesn't have a personal relationship with Jesus? Write their name(s) here.

It took me a while, but I learned a lot about my witness through this experience. I learned that as a man being made into the likeness of God, there's much more to sharing my faith than the outcome. I learned that my witness is an integral part of who I am as a man. And every day, regardless of how others respond, I have a responsibility to live out a life of witness.

The Life You Live > The Words You Say

What if you walked into school this week to find every student and teacher seated in the gymnasium? And what if the principal called you to join him at center court? And then, what if, one by one, every student and teacher in your school walked across the court, grabbed the microphone, and were each given thirty seconds to proclaim to everyone how you've witnessed to them with the way you live your life. What would they say? What would you *want* them to say?

Actions speak louder than words. And people *are* watching. My life is on display for everyone I come in contact with. My family, my close friends, my co-workers, and my neighbors, the person who scans my groceries at Kroger, the waiter who brings me my plate of catfish and pitcher of iced tea at my favorite Nashville restaurant, the people I sit next to on a plane every time I travel, my daughter's soccer coach—every day my life impacts the lives of others. And with each encounter, I have the opportunity—the responsibility—to show them there's something different about me because I'm a follower of Jesus. And often this happens without ever opening my mouth.

The same is true for you. Every day, in every relationship,

with every encounter, you have the chance to be Jesus to your world. Most of the time you don't do it with what you say but with what you do. And for a lot of the people you cross paths with, this could be the only glimpse of God they ever get.

think about it

Does the life your non-Christian friends see you live *with* Jesus differ from the lives they live *without* him?

FORGET THE FEAR FACTOR

Reality TV has proven over and over that people will do crazy things that test their endurance, their faith, and their fears just to get their fifteen minutes of fame.

hit pause

Would you:

- eat a pizza covered in tomato sauce, cheese, and leeches?
- sing really, really badly and be made fun of by judges on national television?
- drink an ice cream smoothie with bananas, strawberries, and bull testicles?

It's amazing how so many people are willing to set aside their fears in pursuit of things that will bring them temporary satisfaction. Imagine what could happen in your life and the lives of those in your world if you set aside your fears, not just to have a moment on TV and a big cash prize, but to see someone's life changed forever.

It took me four months of ignoring what God had asked me to do before I finally chose to share my faith with Eric. Why? Because I was afraid of what Eric might think about me. I was afraid of what Eric might say to me. I was afraid of what Eric might *do* to me...like give me another closeup look at the inside of locker 121.

This is exactly how Satan works. He wants to scare you and me into believing that when we speak to others about God, we'll be ridiculed or picked on. Yes, each of these outcomes is a possibility. But when you choose to let God make you into the man he desires, look at what the Bible says will happen:

> God's Spirit doesn't make cowards out of us. (2 Timothy 1:7, CEV)

As you allow God to work in your life, he'll replace:

your cowardice with courage
your fear with faith
your hesitation with hope
your panic with power
your worry with wonder

When God Asks, He Provides

As you commit to God's plan for your life, get ready. Because along with this commitment comes responsibility—the responsibility to share God with others. In chapter 2 we talked about how you're a man of responsibility. When you start embracing your true role as a man of God by fully submitting your life to him, God will call you to do great things for him. There's no greater privilege in life than sharing the saving message of Jesus with someone else. Sometimes talking to a person about Jesus may seem impossible. But make no mistake, when God calls you to do something:

- He'll *never* require something of you that's impossible.
- He'll *never* require something of you that you have to face alone.

First Corinthians 1:25 says, "Even when God is weak, he is stronger than everyone else" (CEV). Even in God's weakness (of which he has none, by the way), he's still stronger than the greatest human strength. When talking with someone about Jesus, remember, you're not alone. When God asks, he provides:

- the way
- the words
- the courage
- the outcome

the Truth

Jesus looked at them and said, "With man this is impossible, but with God all things are possible." (Matthew 19:26)

A Command, Not a Question

In his final moments on earth before his ascension, Jesus could've chosen any number of directives for us. He chose just one. Check it out:

> Jesus, undeterred, went right ahead and gave his charge: "God authorized and commanded me to commission you: Go out and train everyone you meet, far and near, in this way of life, marking them by baptism in the threefold name: Father, Son, and Holy Spirit. Then instruct them in the practice of all I have commanded you. I'll be with you as you do this, day after day after day, right up to the end of the age." (Matthew 28:18–20, MSG)

Obviously, Jesus thought evangelism was a high priority. Standing atop that mountain, having a conversation man to man with the disciples, Jesus gave a powerful command to those men—and ultimately, to each of us. It was a command to *go.*

hit pause

I know you might be thinking, *Well, I really don't like to be told what to do.* I understand that. I don't always either. But rather than look at it as a command, consider this: you've been given the privilege of sharing the most important, life-changing news with those in your world. That's really not a command. That's a gift. And if you don't talk with your friends about Jesus, who will?

It's Not About You

Remember how I said I was mad at God when he told me to witness to my biggest enemy, who then turned me down when I asked him to accept Jesus? Do you think my feelings were justified? I was mad because things didn't work out the way I wanted them to. But here's the problem—I believed it was *my* responsibility to save Eric. I was carrying the burden, assuming that it was up to me to change Eric's life. And since this didn't happen in the one phone call with him, I thought I'd failed. And when I felt inadequate, I looked for someone to blame. And I blamed God.

In the months that followed, God started to show me it wasn't my responsibility to change Eric, or anyone else for that matter. Because I can't. Only God can do that. God helped me understand that he didn't tell me to go *save* Eric. He just told me to *go*.

hit pause

If you know someone in your life who's not a believer and you haven't talked with them about it, what's keeping you from doing it now?

If you knew that every time you talked to someone about Jesus they would accept him as their personal Savior, would you tell more people about him?

I'm pretty confident your answer would be yes. Why is that? Because you wouldn't have to be afraid of failing or looking stupid. God helped me understand that choosing to talk with someone about him isn't about success or failure. You need to know that if God has laid it on your heart to share his message with someone, then he already has it worked out. Regardless of the immediate outcome, obedience is all that's required of you. You can't control someone's response. All you can control is your obedience.

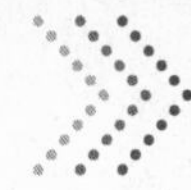

Conversation Starters

- Do you believe there is a God?
- I'd like to tell you how I started a personal relationship with God.
- We're having a youth event at our church. Would you like to come?
- We've been friends for a while, and I've never talked to you about the most important thing in my life. Can I tell you now?
- How do you think someone becomes a Christian?
- What do you think it takes to get into heaven?
- If you were to die tonight, where would you spend eternity?

Understand the Mission

I know someone who's in hell today. At least I think he is. I met this man when I was in college. He told me he didn't believe in God, and he didn't want a relationship with him. He was an alcoholic, and several years later he died a miserable death from a failed liver.

Do you know someone who's not a believer? Have you talked with them about Jesus? Let me be brutally honest for a minute. What I'm about to say won't be easy to read, but this is the real deal: if you know someone who's not a believer, and you choose not to share the saving message of Jesus with them, then it's as if you're saying to them, "Go to hell!"

I know you're probably thinking, *That's pretty harsh, Jeffrey.* You're right. It is harsh. It's also true. If we don't care enough about the people in our lives to share Jesus with them, then we don't care enough to see that they spend eternity with God in heaven. Simply put: we don't care for them enough to try to keep them out of hell.

As you begin to see your interactions with people as opportunities to save them from hell, you'll start to grasp the urgency before you, as a man on a mission, to help change the world. You don't have to stand on a stage to be used in this way. You don't have to write a book, be an American Idol, or do stupid stuff on MTV like Johnny Knoxville in order to have a voice. You just have to understand your mission as a man. This mission isn't about your personal success, popularity, or wealth. It's about your willingness to be used by God to help people step from death to life. It's about saying, "I will go."

It's urgent that you listen carefully to this: Anyone here who believes what I am saying right now and aligns himself with the Father...has at this very moment the real, lasting life and is no longer condemned to be an outsider. This person has taken a giant step from the world of the dead to the world of the living. (John 5:24, MSG)

Know Your Story

There will be many memorable moments in the story of your life. Your first date. Your first car...and your first speeding ticket. Your first pimple. But the greatest moment of the story is the moment you stepped from death to life, from sinner to forgiven, from condemned to transformed. Not only did this moment change you, it can also be a story used to change others, if you'll let it.

The Bible says, "Always be prepared to give an answer to everyone who asks you to give the reason for the hope that you have" (1 Peter 3:15).

Sharing the message of salvation with others isn't rocket science. It's just about being real, being genuine, and being you. You have an incredible story to tell. You have to realize this is true. And you also have to realize that you could be the only light in a friend's life.

No Way

Jeffrey, give me a break. I don't know enough about the Bible to witness to anyone. I'll just screw it up because there's too much I don't know.

I hear you. But there will always be things we don't know. I've been doing this ministry stuff for a long time, and there are still things about the Bible I don't know. Besides, it isn't about having full knowledge of Scripture. It's about sharing what you do know. And what you do know is what God has done *for you* in your own life. Of course, the more Scripture you know, the better prepared you are. John 3:16 is a great verse. So are Romans 10:9 and Romans 10:13. Plus, you'll also find some help in answering a few of the really big questions in the next section of this

chapter. But if someone asks you a question you just don't know the answer to, be honest about your lack of knowledge. Tell your friend that you'll find an answer for them. And then stick to your word. Go talk with a parent or pastor, or go to www.jeffreydean.com and e-mail me. Get an answer to your friend's question, and then go back and share it with them.

Get Your Game Face On

The more you let God change you, the more people will notice a change in you, especially your unsaved friends. They'll see God's character in you. They may notice how you treat others or that you pray before eating lunch at school. Be ready. God will use these moments to bring people to you to share his truth with them. Today you'll most likely come in contact with someone who's not a Christian. Will you be ready?

When you're witnessing, you have to expect some tough questions. Nonbelievers will see you as a representative of Christianity, and they may want you to explain your stance on some of the controversial topics Christians are involved in. You need to be prepared for questions like these. Remember, you don't have to have all the answers to everything (and if you don't know the answer, don't just make something up), but knowing what God's Word says about a few of the big ones will help you be a more effective witness.

Question 1: Is homosexuality wrong?

This is a tough one. It's not so much that the answer is hard to find—there's scripture that states clearly that it's wrong:

> God let them follow their own evil desires. Women no longer wanted to have sex in a natural way, and they did things with each other that were not natural. Men behaved in the same way. They stopped wanting to have sex with women and had strong desires for sex with other men. They did shameful things with each other, and what has happened to them is punishment for their foolish deeds. (Romans 1:26–27, CEV)

It's tough because homosexuality is more accepted in our society now, and saying that it's wrong can make you seem intolerant. And if people think you're intolerant, they're less likely to listen to what you have to say. But you also can't ignore what God's Word says. There's no easy way to handle this. You'll meet people who believe that homosexuals are born with same-sex attraction and that they didn't choose to be gay. You have to know that God didn't create anyone to be homosexual. It's a sin, and it's not part of God's plan. Saying that to someone, however, is not as easy as me writing it in this book.

The best thing to do is remember that you're not anyone's judge. Only God can do that. This will help you be more humble when you share parts of God's Word that aren't so welcome to some people. All you can do when you're faced with issues like homosexuality is let people know what the Bible says—and also let them know that you love them. It may seem impossible to do both at the same time, but God's got a knack for making the impossible possible. All you have to do is ask for his help.

If you know someone who's struggling with homosexuality (it might even be you), and they're not sure what to do about those feelings, you need to let them know they're not alone. Be someone they can talk to. Then tell them they should also talk...

With God: Let them know that God loves them completely. Their struggle is no surprise to him, and he wants to help them break free of it. They should talk to him and ask for strength and guidance.

With Someone Who Will Help: Help them find someone they can trust who will be both honest and kind. Maybe your pastor or youth director or a parent or teacher you know well.

It's important to know that giving in to homosexuality is no more or less wrong than cheating on a test or running a red light. Sin is sin, no matter what sin it is. And God is big enough to handle it and help anyone through it.

Question 2: Are all religions the same?

Not all religions are the same. Some worship false gods. Some believe in God but don't believe that Jesus is his Son. Some believe Jesus was a real person but don't accept the fact that he died for us on the cross and was resurrected from the dead. Some religions don't believe the Bible is the infallible Word of God.

Christianity accepts God as the only God and believes that Jesus is the Son of God, who came to earth, died for humankind, and conquered death by coming back to life and proving that he is the one true Savior of the world. We believe the Bible is God's

Word and the ultimate authority for everything we do. To be a Christian means "one is a follower of Christ."

Christianity is based on a person's willingness to believe in and choose to live for Jesus. Christians believe that faith in Jesus is the only way to get to heaven. You can't just be a good person or just do good deeds (though if you believe in Jesus, you will want to do those things, of course). There's only one path to eternal life, and it's through Jesus. John 14:6 says, "Jesus answered, 'I am the way and the truth and the life. No one comes to the Father except through me.' "

Question 3: Why does God let bad things happen to good people?

"Life's not fair," Jared said in a recent letter to me. "My dad is gone, my mom is depressed, school sucks, and I'm sick of it. I try to do what is right, but nothing seems to go my way!" Can you relate? I know I can. There've been many times in my life when I've had questions about why life can be so unfair. You'll probably ask this a lot too. And you'll most likely have other people ask you this question when they find out you're a Christian.

God has given us a great gift—a gift that people misuse all the time. He's given you and me the free will to live as we please. And because we have the ability to choose, we can often choose the wrong things. So why did God give us the freedom of choice if he knew we could abuse it? God didn't create clones (and aren't you glad he didn't?). He loves us and wants us to love him in return. However, true love can't be forced or manipulated. So since God wanted real love from us, he had to give us the ability to choose. So we can choose to love him…or not love him. And that means we have the freedom to choose to do wrong. Because there's wrong in the world, many bad things happen to people who don't deserve it.

Second (this isn't the easy part to hear), there will be times in life when you have questions you may never have answers for. We'll never fully understand why God does all that he does and allows all that he allows until we reach heaven. The Bible says:

> For who among men knows the thoughts of a man except the man's spirit within him? In the same way no one knows the thoughts of God except the Spirit of God. (1 Corinthians 2:11)

> As you do not know the path of the wind,
> or how the body is formed in a mother's womb,
> so you cannot understand the work of God,
> the Maker of all things. (Ecclesiastes 11:5)

Maybe your mom or dad has left your family or you've lost a loved one or you've been mistreated, abused, or abandoned by someone close to you. When you can't find a good reason for why such things happen, remember that God fully understands your pain. He suffered the greatest injustice of all time: allowing his perfect Son, Jesus, to be arrested, beaten, whipped, spit on, cursed at, and then nailed to a cross to die. He never deserved such treatment. But he did it for you—for all of us.

Remember, whether you're in your rock-star moment or kissing the asphalt of life, God is always on your side. Even when answers to life's troubles are hard (or even impossible) to find, God says, "I will always be with you and help you" (Joshua 1:5, CEV).

Don't Give Up

Talking with Eric about Jesus didn't produce the results I wanted overnight. But God used my willingness to tell Eric my story as a first step in Eric's journey. Sometimes one conversation is all it takes to bring a friend to Jesus. Other times, a lifetime of prayer and patience will be needed. Just as God has never given up on you, don't you give up on anyone.

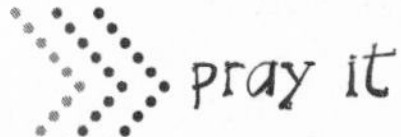

If you're serious about reaching those in your world with the message of Jesus, God will take your request very seriously. Pray that:

- God will give you the opportunity
- God will give you the boldness
- God will give you the words

Everyone you know has one thing in common: they all will go to either heaven or hell. Let God use you to bring those in your life to him. There truly is no greater privilege. Believe me, I know. A year after graduation, Eric found me and told me he had found Jesus. He thanked me for not giving up on him.

How to Talk to a Friend About Jesus

1. Start with your story:

- Who God is to you
- What you believe about God
- What God did for you
- How God changed you

2. Ask questions like:

- Do you believe in God?
- What do you believe about God?
- What confuses you the most about God?

3. Ask the most important question:

- Do you know what it means to ask God into your life? Do you want to ask him to be in your life now?

4. Share the following verses:

- "God loved the people of this world so much that he gave his only Son, so that everyone who has faith in him will have eternal life and never really die." (John 3:16, CEV)

  the point: God loved you enough to let his Son die for you. Even though you're not perfect, he sacrificed his Son in your place so you could still spend eternity with him.

- "All of us have sinned and fallen short of God's glory." (Romans 3:23, CEV)

  the point: We're all sinners. Which means all of us need God's help to get into heaven.

- "Sin pays off with death. But God's gift is eternal life given by Jesus Christ our Lord." (Romans 6:23, CEV) *the point:* Since we're all sinners, we don't deserve to go to heaven. But Jesus died in our place and came back to life. He now offers us the gift of eternal life rather than death.

- "But God showed how much he loved us by having Christ die for us, even though we were sinful." (Romans 5:8, CEV)

  the point: You are so loved by God that he let his Son die in your place, so that you wouldn't have to spend eternity in hell separated from God.

- "So you will be saved, if you honestly say, 'Jesus is Lord,' and if you believe with all your heart that God raised him from death. God will accept you and save you, if you truly believe this and tell it to others." (Romans 10:9–10, CEV)

  the point: If you believe that Jesus died for you and came back to life, and you ask him to save you, he will.

My Space

The more you choose to talk with others about Jesus, the easier it'll become. If there's someone in your life who you know needs him, what will you do about it?

Write a prayer asking God to give you the courage to talk with others about him.

Write the names of these people as a reminder to pray for them and commit to talk to them about God.

1.
2.
3.
4.
5.

12

What's the Purpose?

Every champion needs a plan—plus a secret move or two.

Dear Jeffrey,

I'm seventeen and graduating from high school this year. I have already decided on which college I will attend, but have not declared a major. I haven't been sexually active, partied, or made any huge choices I now regret. I guess you could say that I have done pretty much what I am supposed to do up to this point. But what is bothering me is that I don't feel like I have a purpose in life right now. I have been praying all the time, asking God to show me what he wants for my life but have not received a clear direction from him on my future. I want to do his will, but I can't say that I really know what his will is. How am I supposed to live for God when I am not sure what it is that I have been created to live for? Any advice you can offer me would be great.

Thanks,

—Heath

Heath has a problem I think all of us have at some point. He wants to feel like he has a purpose. Like what he's doing is leading him toward an important goal. Like what he's doing matters.

Clearly understanding your purpose in life, and then knowing how to live out that purpose, isn't always easy. But know this: God doesn't want to keep you in the dark about what you were made to do. His timing may be different from yours, but he wants to reveal more of himself to you daily. And as you grow in him, God's plan for your life will become clearer.

Heath asked me three questions in his letter:

1. Do I have a purpose?
2. How do I know what my purpose is?
3. How do I live out my purpose?

There's nothing wrong with asking these questions—and maybe not getting all the answers right away. What's important is how you choose to handle the search for your purpose. Hopefully my answers to these three questions will help you.

Question 1: Do I Have a Purpose?

We've already discussed this question a little bit in chapter 5. When I explained to you how to obey God, I said that an important part of obedience is believing he has a purpose for you. Do you believe that now? Or are you still not sure?

Some people have to wait much longer than they'd like to find out what their purpose is. And while you're waiting, you can start doubting. If you're still questioning whether God really has a plan for your life, read these verses:

> For everything, absolutely everything, above and below, visible and invisible,... *everything* got started in him and finds its purpose in him. (Colossians 1:16, MSG)

> But with your own eyes
> you saw my body being formed.
> Even before I was born,
> you had written in your book
> everything I would do. (Psalm 139:16, CEV)

> The LORD will fulfill his purpose for me.
> (Psalm 138:8)

You are no accident. Psalm 138:8 proclaims that God will fulfill his purpose for you. You do have a purpose. It's a God-given purpose. And God wants to help you fulfill it. But while you're waiting for your "big" purpose, you also have a purpose that's constant, from the moment you accept Christ until the day you go to live with him in heaven—witnessing to others. I've said it again and again: your greatest privilege—and your greatest responsibility—is to be God's mirror in your world. This is a purpose you don't have to wait for God to reveal to you.

God planned all of creation before time on earth began. Before there was light, animals, food, mountains, oceans, or deserts, God had it all planned out in his heart. And when he dreamed the idea of creation, you were a part of that dream. He dreamed *you.* So no matter how insecure you feel, no matter how unworthy you feel, no matter how afraid you feel, you can't let that stop you from pursuing God's purpose for you. When you're asking and he's not answering, you have to trust he will answer someday. And until then, you have to do all you can for him. You can't sit back and think, *When I lose twenty pounds, then I'll feel better about myself and I'll be able to talk to people about God.* Or *I don't know enough about the Bible yet to do anything for God. Once I know more, then I'll do what he wants.* You're who he made you to be *right now,* and he has things for you to do *right now.* Don't let anything hold you back.

Everything was created through him;
nothing—not one thing!—came into being without him.
What came into existence was Life,
and the Life was Light to live by.
The Life-Light blazed out of the darkness;
the darkness couldn't put it out. (John 1:3–5, MSG)

Question 2: How Do I Know What My Purpose Is?

Wouldn't it be great if every day you received an e-mail from God with specific instructions to get you through the day? How cool would it be if God gave you a road map for the day detailing what you should do, where you should go, who you should talk to, and what you should avoid? It seems like life would be much more manageable that way, doesn't it? Never having to question, think, or make tough decisions. Never second-guessing your choices or wondering, *What if?*

What would happen if today God decided to reveal to you every detail about the rest of your life?

- who you'll marry
- what your occupation will be
- what your children's names will be and what they'll look like
- how those closest to you will die and when
- exactly when, where, and how you'll die

At first, it may seem cool to have an inside scoop on the rest of your life. However, after a while, living that way would also be pretty boring. Life would become nothing more to you than a checklist of events. There would be no wonder, no adventure, no anticipation, and no quest. You'd simply clock in, perform your duties, and then clock out. You'd never be driven to figure anything out or search for the answer or prayerfully seek God's guidance to find the right way to go. Life would be routine and meaningless.

There's a word that perfectly describes the kind of person you would become: *robot.*

God could choose today to give you the blueprints to the rest of your life. And there are times when that offer might seem very tempting. However, when God created you, he didn't create a robot. Instead, he created a *man* who thinks for himself. And remember, being made into the man he desires isn't always easy. And finding your purpose isn't either. But when you do find it, you'll celebrate so much more because you worked to get there instead of just letting God hand you the solution. Until then, though, it'll take time.

Time in the Word

It's impossible to consistently know and do God's will if you don't spend time with him. The Bible is a guide for our lives that God has given us.

Look at Psalm 119:104–105:

> I gain understanding from your precepts....
> Your word is a lamp to my feet
> and a light for my path.

Psalm 119 makes it clear that by spending time in the Word, you'll gain understanding. As you commit to spend time in the Word, you'll develop a greater understanding of who God is. As you begin to know him more, he'll reveal to you a greater understanding of his plan and purpose for your life.

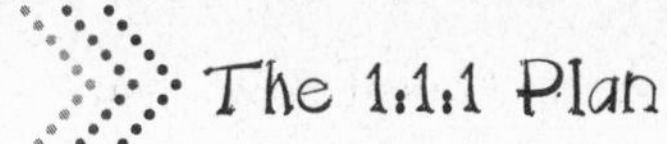

The 1:1:1 Plan

One Passage of Scripture + Once a Day + One Week = Finding Your Purpose

Repetition is key. There are times when I read the Bible and then forget what I read as soon as I walk away. Going back and reading the same verse over will help you absorb the truth of Scripture. And this is the way to live a life that honors God:

> How can a young person live a clean life?
> By carefully reading the map of your Word. (Psalm 119:9, MSG)

Here are some creative ways to spend time in the Word:

1. Grab your Bible and journal, and find your favorite quiet spot—a park, your backyard, or the lake.
2. Go to Starbucks for some Bible and bean time.
3. Get a few friends together for a sleepover, and instead of watching a movie or talking about girls, start a conversation about a scripture you've been reading and encourage each other to spend more time in the Word.
4. Start a Bible club at your school. Commit to meet once a week to dive into the Word and pray together.

Time in Prayer

Write down the answers to the following questions about your closest friend:

- What's their favorite color?
- Who's their favorite musician or band?
- What's their MySpace address?
- How many times have they been to the principal's office?

Have you ever stopped to wonder why you know so much about the people in your life who are important to you? The reason is, you've made it a priority to spend time with those people. In short, time = knowledge.

The same is true when it comes to your relationship with God. You'll know him better as you spend time talking with him. When you do, he'll reveal himself to you in ways he never has before. And the more time you invest in your relationship with God, the more important your relationship with him will become to you.

Look at what Mark 11:24 says:

> That's why I urge you to pray for absolutely everything, ranging from small to large. Include everything as you embrace this God-life, and you'll get God's everything. (MSG)

Mark 11:24 says it all: embrace a life of prayer with God, and God will give you everything.

Have an Awesome Prayer Life

1. Escape

   Prayer can happen anytime, anywhere. But choosing a specific place to escape to, away from distractions, can help you focus on God and not on the busyness of your life.

2. Schedule

   Strive to develop a habit of praying at the same time each day. Log it on your PDA, phone, or laptop, and treat prayer just like a daily meeting. If you're not a morning person, don't sweat it. Make your prayer time an afternoon thing after school or in the evening before bed. There's no right or wrong way to do it. Find out what works for you, and stick to it.

3. Shuffle

   Shuffle your prayer experience. One day pray for yourself, the next pray for someone at school, then a family member, then a friend—you get the point.

4. Journal

   Keeping a prayer journal is a great way to keep your prayer life organized. This'll remind you of specific things you want to pray for and help you see how God answers so many of your prayers.

5. Talk

   Talk to God like you would talk to your best friend over coffee.

Time Listening to God

Consider all the things you listen to:

- music
- friends
- MTV
- your dog (questionable…)
- parents

Now consider how much time to you spend listening to God. As we discussed in chapter 5, God wants to talk to you. Proverbs 1:5 says, "Let the wise listen and add to their learning, and let the discerning get guidance." Choosing to listen to God will help you gain understanding of the purpose he's created you for.

give it a shot

A high-school boy named Christopher told me that his drive time to school is typically the time when he pops in his favorite CD. In his effort to spend more time talking and listening to God, he made a commitment to spend the first half of his twenty-minute drive listening to music and the second half praying and listening to God. He explained that applying this to his morning commute has been a positive way to start living a God-focused day. Find a little window in your life to give over to God. Just a small amount of time spent with him will make a big difference.

Time Waiting

We live in an instant-message, ATM, DSL, drive-through, got-to-have-it-now world. Waiting isn't always fun. And sometimes it really stinks. But God says sometimes waiting is a necessary part of realizing our true purpose in life.

Moses waited 40 years before fulfilling his purpose to help lead the Israelites out of captivity. Noah built an ark and waited 120 years before it ever floated. David waited many sleepless nights, hiding in caves and running for his life, before becoming the greatest king in the history of Israel.

God may choose to reveal to you the fullness of his plan and purpose for your life in the next five minutes, five years, or fifty years. But no matter how long the wait, choosing to wait faithfully will be much easier for you than choosing to wait miserably. But this is a difficult step to master. You have to focus on the reward that God says comes to those who choose to wait for him:

> Yet those who wait for the LORD
> Will gain new strength;
> They will mount up with wings like eagles,
> They will run and not get tired,
> They will walk and not become weary.
> (Isaiah 40:31, NASB)

If, like Heath, you find yourself frustrated over the uncertainty of your future, be encouraged. You're never alone. We'll have times when we're anxious to know where we're headed in life. And God understands how you feel. Rather than have you frustrated by the uncertainty, he wants you to use this time to rely on him even more. I know that waiting isn't on your list of favorite things to do, but learning patience is essential if you want to grow as a Christian. It could be that God has you right here in this moment because he too is waiting—waiting to have your undivided attention, waiting patiently for you to give him all of yourself.

The waiting process may make you feel like a little kid lying in bed on Christmas Eve, anxiously anticipating the arrival of Santa Claus—and all the gifts he has for you. But really, waiting isn't a passive process. It requires action on your part. Which leads to the final question Heath asked in his letter.

Question 3: How Do I Live Out My Purpose?

First, be confident. Remember that one of the Foundational Truths of this book is: God's Word is truth. If he says it, he means it. Look at the promise God gives you in Philippians 1:6:

> Being confident of this, that he who began a good work in you will carry it on to completion until the day of Christ Jesus.

In his letter, it's obvious Heath is struggling with believing that God created him with a purpose. Heath assumed that because God had not fully disclosed this purpose to him yet, there was no purpose at all. You may be in Heath's position right now. It may not be time for God to fully reveal his plan to you. However, you can confidently move forward one day at a time believing that God will finish what he started when he created you. And you can know that, while you're waiting, you have the daily purpose of being Jesus to every person you meet.

You may be thinking, *Jeffrey, how am I supposed to live out my faith confidently when I don't even really know what my purpose is?* Well, that's a great question. And fortunately, I have a great answer for it:

Living out your purpose requires tremendous faith.

Be firm in your faith.
Stay brave and strong.
(1 Corinthians 16:13, CEV)

Check out what Hebrews 11:1 says: "Faith makes us sure of what we hope for and gives us proof of what we cannot see" (CEV).

Even when you don't have all the answers, and even when the direction you should go in life is about as clear as mud, you've got to be willing to trust God if you want to find and live out his plan for your life. Even when it doesn't make sense. And even when it doesn't feel fair.

I know the word *faith* can be difficult to adequately define. For me, living a life of faith means that I strive every day to live more for God than I did the previous day. And tomorrow, I'll work to repeat that process.

The older I get, the more I realize that finding and living out God's plan for our lives isn't necessarily about arriving at a destination. Rather, it's more about a journey. With every step we should become more like him, and every day we should surrender more of ourselves to him. When we walk that path, our formation—our transformation—can continue.

I guess you could say then that the process of becoming the

man God made you to be doesn't end until you breathe your last breath. I think that's what Paul was describing in Ephesians 4:13 when he said, "This will continue until we are united by our faith and by our understanding of the Son of God. Then we will be mature, just as Christ is, and we will be completely like him" (CEV).

No Way

So, you've made me read almost this entire book just to tell me that becoming the man God wants me to be is something that never ends. I'll never actually become that man until I die? That's not what I wanted to hear. It almost sounds like things would be easier on my own.

Okay, I know at first it sounds pretty tough...and even disappointing. But really it's nice to know that, as long as you live, God's working in you to make you better. You never get to a point where God's like, "That's all I can do with you. This is as good as you'll get." There's always more good stuff to come. I know I'm still learning and growing in my relationship with God. I definitely don't have it all figured out yet. But I finally came to a point in my life where I was willing to completely surrender it all to him. I'm trying really hard to trust where he has me today and where he wants to take me tomorrow.

I guess...but that sounds kind of exhausting and scary.

Sure, it can be. But knowing I'm being made into something bigger than I'll ever become on my own helps me to remove the fear and just embrace the journey. Plus, God never makes mistakes, so what he's offering may sound hard, but the outcome will be better than anything you can do on your own.

Hear me clearly: It is *not* always easy to live the way I've described, especially when we live in a world that's trying to pull us away from God. So when you fail, don't beat yourself up. Just get back up and start again. Remember, being made into the man he desires is not about perfection. It's about consistency.

My Space

What do you believe God is asking you to do with your life this year?

What one thing is God showing you that you need to do to grow in your relationship with him?

Write a prayer asking God to help you commit to this one thing.

Freakin' Fearless

Here's your chance to show the world what God can do through you.

I love scary movies. Not the ones with blood, guts, and a psycho, but the ones with suspense, mystery, and a twist at the end that hits you upside the head out of nowhere. You know, like the last ten minutes of *The Village.* Or the final minutes in *The Sixth Sense.* And, of course, the full hour and a half of one of the greatest mystery movies of all time, *Scooby Doo*—the one where the mystery gang reunites on an island to investigate strange occurrences. Don't play dumb...you know you watched it.

Anyway, though you may not be a *Scooby Doo* fan, I bet you've seen a few movies that have left you freaked. But it's not just movies that scare us. Real life can be pretty frightening too. Choosing to live as a stander rather than a sitter will mean there'll be a lot of times when you're afraid—moments when it seems like you're the only one standing for what's right.

Obviously, God knew this would happen. That's why 2 Timothy 1:7 says, "God gave us a spirit not of fear but of power" (ESV).

However, sometimes it's hard to know that spirit is there. Look at what one guy wrote to me:

> Jeffrey,
>
> You spoke at my summer camp last year. I have never been challenged by anyone the way that you challenged all of us there. I am trying to apply the things to my life that you encouraged us to do. But the fact is, it's difficult to live a life that honors God, especially at school. It seems like there aren't very many people in my school who say they are Christians. And even the few who say they are don't really live like it. I know that taking a stand for God is what is right, but sometimes it feels like I am the only one standing.

Sadly, this will be the case more times than you'd like. When I was younger, there were a lot of times when I felt like I was the only person in my school standing for what was right. Have you ever felt this way? I bet you have a time or two...or three hundred. And if you haven't yet, get ready, because living out God's purpose for your life will inevitably lead to some stand-alone moments.

It really stinks to feel like you're standing all by yourself on the right side of the fight with everyone staring at you like you're crazy. But you won't be the last to do it—and you definitely won't be the first. The Bible is chockfull of stories about people who stood up for God when no one else would. And the one you probably know best is the story of David and Goliath.

We all know about David, how he conquered Goliath with a slingshot and became one of the greatest kings in the history of Israel. He was a mighty warrior, a strong leader, extremely wealthy, and greatly respected by many. But long before any of these accomplishments became a reality, David was just a teenager, waiting to live out his purpose. You may've heard this story a million times, but this time let's focus on who David was when he walked out onto that field with a rock in hand. Because he was just a normal kid when God called him. Just like you.

There are lots of ways people might describe David. Because he's one of the Bible's greatest heroes, people imagine him as a handsome Brad Pitt type, but with more muscles, like a pro wrestler or something. Or they think he's quick and smart, like Peyton Manning is on the football field. But when David puts a dent in Goliath's skull, he's really none of those things. If I could think of a contemporary example, I wouldn't pick any handsome, suave, perfect guy. I'd pick Napoleon Dynamite. Yes, you read that right—Napoleon Dynamite.

Like Napoleon, David was underappreciated by those who knew him as a teenager, even by his brothers and his father. He spent a lot of time writing songs on his harp while tending his sheep, so he probably didn't have a ton of friends. Oh, and also, David did a crazy dance in front of everyone (and his wife made fun of him for it). Check out 2 Samuel 6 for the details on David's moves.

So what about this David and Goliath story? It almost seems too cliché to have any relevance for you. But if you really try to imagine David as a guy like you, a little awkward, maybe uncool or even nerdy, the story starts to look a little different. First

Samuel 17:4, 8–11 gives us a clear picture of the scene before young David steps in. From this description, it sounds like no one can save Israel, especially not a kid like him—or like you.

> The Philistine army had a hero named Goliath who was from the town of Gath and was over nine feet tall....
>
> Goliath went out and shouted to the army of Israel:
>
> > Why are you lining up for battle? I'm the best soldier in our army, and all of you are in Saul's army. Choose your best soldier to come out and fight me! If he can kill me, our people will be your slaves. But if I kill him, your people will be our slaves. Here and now I challenge Israel's whole army! Choose someone to fight me!
>
> Saul and his men heard what Goliath said, but they were so frightened of Goliath that they couldn't do a thing. (CEV)

So King Saul and the Israelites are camped on one side of the hill in the Valley of Elah, and Goliath and his boys are on the other. The Bible says David shows up at the battle site to check on his brothers, who are warriors in King Saul's army. David isn't old enough or strong enough to be a soldier himself, but when he hears Goliath running his mouth, he talks like he's the leader of the army.

> "Your Majesty," [David] said, "this Philistine shouldn't turn us into cowards. I'll go out and fight him myself!"

"You don't have a chance against him," Saul replied. "You're only a boy, and he's been a soldier all his life."

But David told him:

> Your Majesty, I take care of my father's sheep. And when one of them is dragged off by a lion or a bear, I go after it and beat the wild animal until it lets the sheep go. If the wild animal turns and attacks me, I grab it by the throat and kill it.
>
> Sir, I have killed lions and bears that way, and I can kill this worthless Philistine. He shouldn't have made fun of the army of the living God! The Lord has rescued me from the claws of lions and bears, and he will keep me safe from the hands of this Philistine.

"All right," Saul answered, "go ahead and fight him. And I hope the LORD will help you." (1 Samuel 17:32–37, CEV)

Up until this point in his life, David was a nobody. Just a weird kid who hung out with sheep. Yeah, one day he'd be a great king, but he wasn't even close to wearing a crown when he basically said, "Watch this! I can kick this humongous guy into next week!" Where did he get the courage to say stuff like that, anyway?

David Knew He'd Won Before the Battle Even Began

When Goliath saw that David was just a healthy, good-looking boy, he made fun of him. "Do you think I'm a

> dog?" Goliath asked. "Is that why you've come after me with a stick?... Come on! When I'm finished with you, I'll feed you to the birds and wild animals!"
>
> David answered:
>
> > You've come out to fight me with a sword and a spear and a dagger. But I've come out to fight you in the name of the LORD All-Powerful....
> >
> > Today the LORD will help me defeat you. I'll knock you down and cut off your head, and I'll feed the bodies of the other Philistine soldiers to the birds and wild animals....
>
> When Goliath started forward, David ran toward him. He put a rock in his sling and swung the sling around by its straps. When he let go of one strap, the rock flew out and hit Goliath on the forehead. It cracked his skull, and he fell facedown on the ground. David defeated Goliath with a sling and a rock. He killed him without even using a sword. (1 Samuel 17:42–50, CEV)

David was able to be so brave because he knew he had God on his side. And talk about confidence! David was freakin' fearless. He stared Goliath in the face and declared war. Before he ever threw his first rock, David knew he'd won because he trusted the Lord that much.

When you've accepted Christ, you've already won too. You might not defeat guys way bigger than you—that might not be God's plan for you. But you've always got the winning hand, even when it looks like you're losing. Why? Because, just like David, you have God on your side. David was the youngest and, for most of his life, least respected in his family, but all that time he was winning, because God was preparing him for great things. God was pulling for David. And he's pulling for you. David wasn't afraid. And you don't have to be either.

DAVID STOOD WHEN NO ONE ELSE WOULD

Everyone on that hillside had been shaking in their tents for the last forty days. Verse 24 says that "when the Israelite soldiers saw Goliath, they were scared and ran off" (CEV). But not David. His faith made him fearless. And he was the only one willing to stand for what was right that day.

Living as a man in pursuit of God's will for your life can be a scary thing. I know. I've been there, done that, read the book, and seen the movie. When life seems unfair, or things don't go your way, or it seems as though no one else in your world gives a rip about God, this is when Satan works fast and furious to scare you into doing the wrong thing.

In a moment of fear, the lies are near:

- "Don't stand. You'll be the only one."
- "Go ahead, join in. It's just this one time."
- "If you don't join them, you'll be left out."
- "You don't really think you can stand up, do you? Don't do it—you'll lose."

In these moments, it can be easy to question God's intentions and wonder why you're the only one willing to stand. Sometimes the circumstances of your life may seem unfair. And there'll be times when you're faced with a question about life's circumstances that doesn't have an immediate answer.

But remember: Being fearless doesn't mean you'll have all the answers. It just means that you're willing to step out in the midst of questions because you trust that God has all the answers.

give it a shot

The next time you feel like you're the only one willing to stand, remember that there could be many more sitting around, wanting to stand too, but they need someone else—you—to take the lead. Give it a shot and stand.

David stood when no one else would. He seized the opportunity. He didn't shy away from it. And victory would soon be his.

David Wasn't Concerned with What Others Thought

No one believed that David had it in him to conquer Goliath. Even his own brother made fun of him:

> David's oldest brother Eliab heard him talking with the soldiers. Eliab was angry at him and said, "What are you doing here, anyway? Who's taking care of that little flock of sheep out in the desert? You spoiled brat! You came here just to watch the fighting, didn't you?" (1 Samuel 17:28, CEV)

King Saul questioned his abilities too:

> "You don't have a chance against him," Saul replied.
> "You're only a boy, and he's been a soldier all his life."
> (1 Samuel 17:33, CEV)

It could be that there is someone in your life, maybe even a close family member, who doesn't recognize the many strengths you possess. Don't let their lack of belief in you keep you from believing in yourself. David didn't let his brother or the king shake his confidence. Living fearlessly is about living in confidence and having faith that God has your back. This book has given you a list of qualities that define you as a man. In moments of doubt and times of temptation, use that list to remind yourself of who you are. And then believe it.

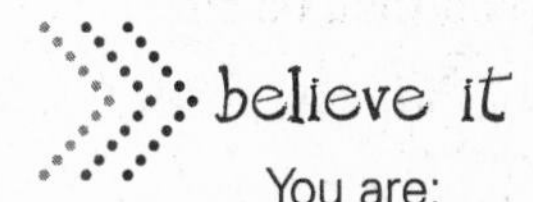

You are:

- a stander
- not a sitter
- an image bearer of God
- good
- a man of responsibility
- not a hider
- a man of commitment
- a man of purpose

As a freshman in high school, I didn't weigh very much. I was skinny and covered in pimples, and my nose seemed to grow at a much faster rate than the rest of my body. I wasn't very athletic, and throughout high school I had to work hard to make average grades. On the other hand, my older brother was the coolest kid on campus—he was popular, smart, and very athletic. He lettered in basketball, football, and track every year of high school. He was vice president of his senior class and was chosen Mr. Robinson High School his senior year. I, on the other hand, graduated high school as a very underconfident man. I was already partway through college when I began to truly understand who I was:

> You are the ones chosen by God, chosen for the high calling of priestly work, chosen to be a holy people, God's instruments to do his work and speak out for him, to tell others of the night-and-day difference he made for you—from nothing to something, from rejected to accepted. (1 Peter 2:9–10, MSG)

David was dwarfed by that great giant from Gath. Unlike his brothers, who were much older and were warriors in Israel's army, David's daily responsibilities amounted to nothing more than running around a field, taking care of sheep. Up until this point in his life, David definitely wouldn't have been asked to appear on the cover of *Israelites Illustrated.* And had you lined up all the warriors in Saul's army that day, David would've probably been considered the most unlikely candidate for the job. But none of that stopped David from living fearlessly. He knew who he was, and he was ready to fight for what he believed in. And he didn't allow others' perceptions of him, or the fact that he didn't possess a strong résumé, to get in the way of God's using him to do something incredible with his life.

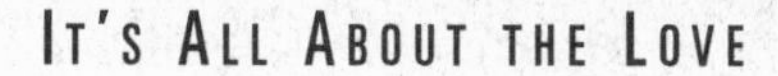

It's All About the Love

As we've discussed often throughout this book, you have to do your part. You've got to be proactive. David didn't wait alongside his brothers, King Saul, and the rest of the wimpy warriors in the Israelite army. He stood fearlessly. And the rest is history.

You may be thinking, *Yes, but come on, Jeffrey, this is a story about a guy who did right and God rewarded him. My story isn't so pretty. I haven't always honored God with my life.*

Well, if you'd read on about the story of David's life, you'd see that David did some pretty disgusting things. Later on, he lusted after another man's wife, had an affair with her, got her pregnant, tried to trick her husband into sleeping with her so that he would think it was his baby, then eventually had him killed to try to cover up the whole thing. Yet, of all the great men whose stories fill the pages of the Bible, David is the only man God says is "a man after his own heart" (1 Samuel 13:14).

Whoa! Stop the press. Rewind. Could this be true? God actually said that a lusting, cheating, lying, deceiving murderer is a man after his own heart? Yes. It's true. On the battlefield in front of others, David was the man. In his private life, behind closed doors, David made some horrible mistakes. But God still chose to use David to do great things for him. The point is, if God can use David, even after all the mistakes he made, God can use you too.

Remember, the ultimate goal of being made into the man God desires isn't perfection. It's about becoming a man after God's own heart—someone who wants to be more like God every day. David's life story shows that God's not in the business of using perfect people. God's in the business of using imperfect people to fulfill his perfect plan. People willing to set aside their fears—and stand.

think about it

Are you a man after God's own heart?

If yes, in what ways?

If not, what can you do to change that?

A heart like God's:

- chooses God's ways, even when they're not popular
- looks for a way out in a moment of temptation

- strives to please God in all things
- wants to reflect Christ in everything he does
- realizes his mistake, confesses it to God, and gets back on the horse and starts riding again

Watch This

There're so many things in this world I don't understand. I don't get why there have to be mosquitoes or why people get zits or why the dobsonfly exists. (*What's the dobsonfly,* you ask? It's a weird little bug that stays in a dormant larval stage for years, and then when it hatches, it dies just a few days later. How can anyone make sense of that?) And I'll never, ever fully understand girls—even though I have a family full of them now.

I don't understand why God let Herod kill so many innocent babies in the Bible or why Adolf Hitler was allowed to murder millions of Jews. Why does he allow tornadoes to take innocent lives, child molesters to get away with what they do, and thousands to die in terrorist attacks? It's all a mystery to me.

But there's one thing I do know. God *does* have all the answers, and if you trust him, then you don't need to know it all—because you know that he knows. There's no one better to have on your side than the One who knows everything. Awkward, forgotten little David knew that. And that's why he stepped out and conquered Goliath, even when everyone thought he was just plain delusional.

When you're a man after God's own heart, every day the doubters of the world will try to keep you from standing. Immorality will try to trip you up and make you feel unworthy.

And there'll be giant-size odds staring you in the face, telling you there's no way you can win.

So what're you going to do? You can sit comfortably on the sidelines, and it may seem easy and safe there. But it'll also be dull—and unfulfilling.

Or you can be like David and realize you were made for more.

Anyone can be a sitter. And you can probably find a million reasons why that's all you should be. I'm sure David had a long list of reasons why he couldn't defeat Goliath. But he traded that in for the one reason he could—God.

You haven't been called to sit. You're a stander. So stand up and step out. Don't look back. Look forward. Get ready to show everyone what God can do through you.

And be freakin' fearless when you say:

"Watch this."